MAKING AND
CO-ORDINATING
CURTAINS
&
CUSHIONS

MAKING AND CO-ORDINATING
CURTAINS
&
CUSHIONS

MYRA DAVIDSON

B.T. Batsford Ltd · London

A QUARTO BOOK
First published in Great Britain by
B. T. Batsford Ltd.
4 Fitzhardinge Street, London
W1H 0AH

ISBN 0-7134-7389-4

A catalogue record for this book is
available from the British Library

This book was designed and produced by
Quarto Publishing plc
6 Blundell Street
London N7 9BH

Senior Editor Honor Head
Senior Art Editor Amanda Bakhtiar
Designer Alyson Kyles
Illustrators Sharon Smith, with
additional artwork supplied by
Elsa Godfrey, Rob Shone
Photographer Paul Forrester,
Chas Wilder
Publishing Director Janet Slingsby
Art Director Moira Clinch
Picture Manager Rebecca Horsewood
Picture Researcher Anna Kobryn

Typeset in Great Britain by
Servis Filmsetting Ltd, England
Manufactured by Regent Publishing
Services Ltd
Printed by Leefung-Asco Printers Ltd,
China

CONTENTS

SETTING A STYLE

Before choosing colours and materials for soft furnishings for your home, you need to decide on the style you wish to create. This section gives guidance on the considerations to bear in mind when choosing a style that will suit your home, your family and your lifestyle. Advice is given on how to achieve a fully co-ordinated look as well as practical suggestions on how to create the desired effect.

SETTING A STYLE

CREATING A SUCCESSFUL look by co-ordinating colours, patterns and textures is great fun and has endless possibilities, but a mistake can be costly as well as disappointing and can ruin the whole look. To try to avoid this it is useful to know a little about the very basics of interior design – this will help you to make the right sort of judgements when deciding to match or contrast to create a certain look.

The only way to begin is by considering the room you want to decorate. Try to look at it as dispassionately as possible, and consider the amount of natural daylight it receives, its basic size and shape, and the number, shape and type of windows. See whether there are good features which you may want to enhance, or ugly ones such as radiators, runs of pipes, or large built-in items which you want to disguise.

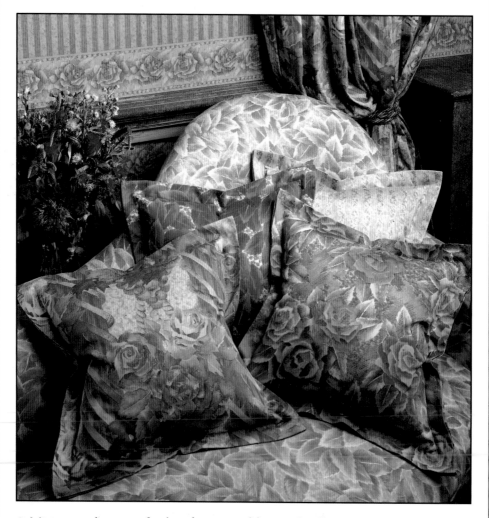

▲ *Mixing complementary florals and stripes on fabrics and wallcovering gives immediate impact.*

▲ *Cushions and bedding in understated colours soften a minimalist bedroom.*

You will also need to consider the way you use the room, its purpose and function – and your family requirements. This may restrict your choice of colour and surface treatments – there is no point in using pale colours, fragile textures and flowing drapes in a well-used family room, although you might get away with them in an "adults only" sitting room or bedroom.

This is where colour, pattern, texture and fabric will come to your aid. The colours you choose for the window treatments, soft furnishings, accents and accessories will give a room ambience and atmosphere, and help you to produce a specific period flavour. Colour is the first thing you notice about a room.

Pattern and texture set the style and can help create a modern, ethnic or period flavour. Fabric helps to complete the chosen look and add interest.

CREATING WITH COLOUR

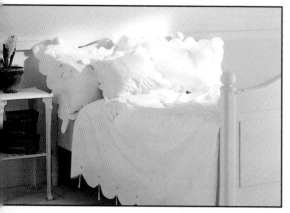

▲ *White and neutrals create a calm, restful mood for a bedroom.*

Basically there are two types of colour: the cool or receding ones, which seem to go away from you, and the warm or advancing ones, which appear to come towards you. The cool colours are the blues, blue-greens, greens, blue-lilacs and blue-greys. They will create a calm atmosphere and make a space look larger, especially if you use pale tones on the main surfaces. But they can give a room a chilly feel, so are best in sunny rooms. The warm colours are the reds, pinks, oranges and yellows, and reddish or pinkish browns.

Neutral colours

There is also the range of "non" colours – the neutrals. The only true neutrals are black, white and grey, but there is a large range of what are sometimes called "coloured neutrals" – beiges, creams, mushrooms, off-whites, and the natural colours of woods, cane, marble, brick, stone, raw wool, flax, undyed cotton and so on. They generally act as a link or background to a scheme, although they can be used on their own to create a restrained and relaxing atmosphere. It is essential to add plenty of variety in texture with neutral colours.

▲ *Stimulating, contrasting orange and blue are softened with neutral beige.*

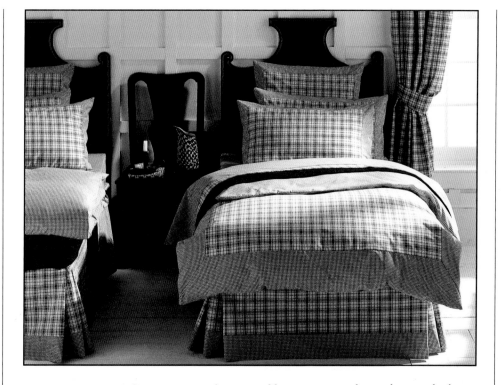

▲ *Strong, warm, red accents add interest to a cool, mainly neutral scheme.*

Colour accents

One secret of the interior decorator's craft well worth knowing is the introduction of contrasting accent colours into a scheme. If you opt for a mainly pale, cool scheme, or a neutral one, add a few touches of rich, bright, hot colours; if you decide on rich, warm shades, add some sharp, cool contrasts. These accents can be provided by trimmings on curtain tie-backs, pelmets and valances; cushions and placemats in the dining-room and valances and throw-over covers in the bedroom.

Harmony and contrast

Just as there are two basic types of colour, there are two basic types of colour scheme – those that rely on harmony and those that make use of contrast.

A harmonious scheme is one where colours next to each other on a colour wheel are used, for example a room decorated in blues and mauves would be harmonious. Such schemes are usually easy to live with, and can create a warm or cool atmosphere, or be a mixture of both, depending on the section of the colour wheel chosen.

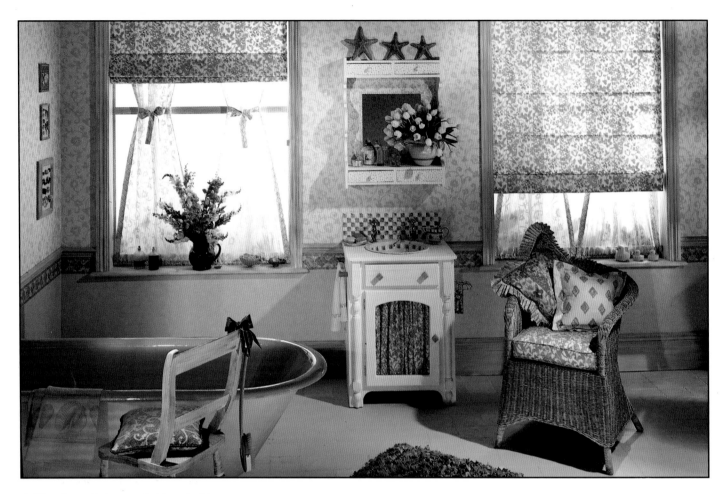

▲ *Blue for cool elegance is teamed with sunny yellow to add a warm touch to an evocative Edwardian bathroom.*

▲ *To colour match the professional way collect some suitable-sized samples and look at them under day and night lighting.*

Colour matching

If you want to get colour scheming right, tackle colour matching in a professional way. This means taking examples of existing items with you when you search for the rest of the scheme. If you have decided on a curtain fabric, for example, take a piece with you when you are choosing the material for contrasting accessories or for paint or wall coverings, to check the exact colour. If this is not possible, bring home a paint manufacturer's colour card or swatch and hold it against the existing items. Don't forget to match up to built in furniture such as kitchen units and worktops.

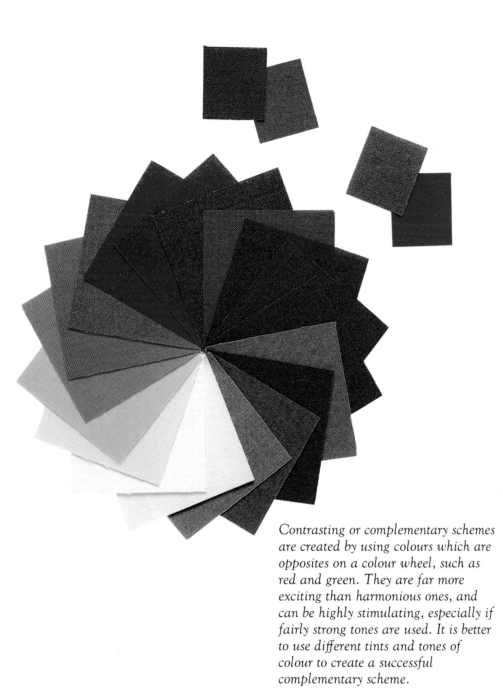

Contrasting or complementary schemes are created by using colours which are opposites on a colour wheel, such as red and green. They are far more exciting than harmonious ones, and can be highly stimulating, especially if fairly strong tones are used. It is better to use different tints and tones of colour to create a successful complementary scheme.

Collect samples of the other items which you propose to use in the room and bring them home. If you are trying to judge the effect of a strong colour or bold pattern, try to get as large a sample as possible. Make all the pieces into a colour or sample board by pinning them to a rigid piece of card and look at them in the room where you propose to use them, first in daylight and then in artificial light – lighting conditions affect colours dramatically – they can look quite different – and you may find that a scheme which looks lovely in daylight doesn't work in artificial light.

COLOUR SCHEMING – A FEW BASIC RULES

• Relate colour schemes to the room – consider size, shape and aspect.

• Use warm colours for an intimate, cosy effect; cool ones for a spacious elegant look.

• Scheme cold rooms mainly in warm colours; warm ones in cool colours.

• Decorate large rooms in strong, rich or dark warm colours – use some bold pattern.

• Choose light, cool colours to make a small room more spacious – use discreet or small-scale patterns.

• Use neutral colours as a link, or to tone down a too-strong scheme.

• Introduce sharp colour contrasts or accents for emphasis; add warm ones to a cool scheme; cool ones in a warm room; clear, bright ones to a neutral scheme.

• Don't use all light colours, or all dark ones – achieve a balance by mixing light, dark and mid-tones.

• Bright, deep, strong colours as well as bold designs and jazzy patterns look bolder used over a large area. Pale or muted colours and small patterns look quieter, and can almost fade into insignificance when used in bulk.

PATTERN AND TEXTURE

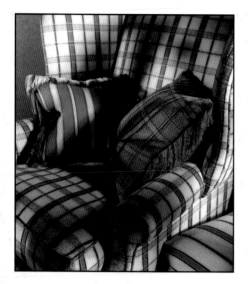

SUCCESSFUL DECORATING and soft furnishing schemes do not rely on colour alone – patterns used on the various surfaces play an essential part too. Both add an extra dimension to a scheme and will help you to play some visual decorating "tricks".

Patterns

Bold patterns, for example, are like warm colours – they seem to come towards you, and thus will be very dominant. They will make a large area seem smaller and more intimate, but if you use them in too small a space walls will appear to close in. Bold patterns also create a "busy" and stimulating atmosphere – good for halls, family rooms and children's rooms, but less good for the main surfaces in a room where you want to relax.

Small and mini-print patterns are like cool colours – they seem to pull away from you. They can appear rather bland unless the colour scheme is a particularly interesting one, but they are useful for creating an impression of space in a small area – also use them if you want a relaxing, calm atmosphere.

Size and scale

In order for pattern to work successfully you need to relate the scale of the pattern to the area over which it is to be used. Bold designs look good up at large windows, on unbroken walls, or over big tables where the full impact can be appreciated. If you use them for small windows or wall areas or as cushion covers the impact of the pattern will be lost. Similarly, small patterns are lost if they are used on large areas, so reserve these for broken-up wall areas and neat, short curtains and blinds and smaller cushions.

If you find choosing a decorating scheme difficult, collect pictures from magazines and catalogues. Or take something you like as a "key" – perhaps a patterned, multi-coloured piece of upholstery or curtain fabric – and echo the various colours on the other surfaces in the room. For example, a floral curtain fabric patterned in greens, golds, pinks and reds on a cream ground can be echoed in pink walls, cream woodwork, green floor, red and gold upholstery piped in green.

If you have several plain surfaces which you want to unify, link them with a patterned item incorporating all the colours. This could be used

◄ *Stripes and checks combine to create a smart tailored look on cushions and curvaceous chair; shaggy fringes edge the cushions to soften the angular shape.*

► *Softly-printed patterns on fabrics and walls rely on textural contrast for impact; glazed chintz emphasizes the quality of the painted woodwork.*

on a main surface or introduced in accessories such as cushions. It could be a patterned pelmet or valance topping plain drapes, or a fabric border used to trim covers and curtains.

Begin with the main pattern and work up the scheme from there – remember a design looks more "fluid" and interesting when made up into curtains, which are softly draped, and can also seem quite different when drawn back to each side of the window.

Textures

Texture is as important as colour and pattern. There are several different types of texture – try to achieve a balance between them just as carefully as when choosing a pattern and plain "mix".

Shiny textures – metals, glass, ceramic tiles, marble, gloss and vinyl silk paint, glazed and silky fabrics – all bounce light back at you. They may make a space seem larger, but they can also look chilly. A room with too many shiny surfaces can be uncomfortable to live in, but some glossy textures are essential for stimulation and contrast.

▲ *Natural wood and rough rustic brickwork add warmth to the tiled window area, offset by chintz drapes and sheer light-filtering café curtains.*

▶ *Crunchy lace topping over net sheers screens a classic window while brass poles, marble floor tiles and matt-painted walls emphasize the elegant outline of the wooden chair.*

Rough, shaggy and soft textures – long and looped-pile carpets, sisal, coir and rush matting, brick and stone, cork, unvarnished wood, coarsely woven fabrics, velvets and wool, and matt and rough-cast paints all absorb light, making the surfaces seem duller, more subtle – or in some cases richer.

They create a calm and more relaxing atmosphere, working like the receding colours and quiet patterns. A room with lots of soft and rough textures can be very comfortable and cosy, but can also be stifling – again good textural contrast is needed to offset them.

Light-filtering textures – lace, nets, muslin, voiles, open-weave sheers, slatted and rattan blinds, etc. – all allow the light to pass through while at the same time diffusing it. This gives a fragile, delicate or ethereal quality, and will make the colour look paler.

▲ *Damask and ticking, flock wall-covering and rich mahogany all create a period flavour, enhanced by matching the cushion and chair seat covers.*

VISUAL TRICKS WITH TEXTURE AND PATTERN

• **To make an area look larger and lighter** – use small patterns; "open", geometric prints, which give a greater impression of space; unifying pattern on wall and windows. Pick shiny light-reflecting textures for walls, ceilings and woodwork; use sheer fabrics or slatted blinds at the windows; add some shiny metal in furniture or accessories.

• **To make a space seem smaller** – use bold patterns on the main surfaces; contrasting pattern on walls and windows; choose strongly patterned upholstery, bedcovers and tablecloths to contrast with floor and walls. Select rough, soft, shaggy and other light-absorbing textures for floor, wall and window treatments; lots of contrasting effects.

• **To add height to a room** – use strong vertical stripes and patterns for wall and window treatments; bold plain curtains or blinds to contrast with the wall.

• **To lower a too-tall ceiling** – put bold horizontal patterns on the walls in wallcoverings or cladding; use a dado/picture rail/frieze/cornice treatment to create strong horizontal architectural features; use similar patterns, slatted shutters or louvres at windows.

• **To add width to a narrow room** – use bold linear patterns widthwise across the floor. Or use light and dark tiles laid in a chequerboard fashion; select horizontal wall and window treatments as above.

• **To shorten a long room** – use bold patterns on the narrow ends (could be curtains at one end with co-ordinating wallcovering or a "dress" curtain at the other); break up floor area with defined patterns – a rug or borders going across the room; use contrasting textures – rugs on boards, lino, ceramics or vinyl.

• **To hide ugly features** – use pattern as camouflage – cover all the surfaces with the same bold design; use light-absorbing textures.

• **To emphasize attractive features** – contrast pattern with plain, using a bold pattern against a richly textured plain background; use light-reflecting textures on the feature you want to emphasize.

FABRIC FACTS

BEFORE YOU SET out to choose a fabric it is essential to consider, as well as the colour and pattern, the type of wear it will get, the "handle" or draping quality, the ease of care and cleaning, and the safety factor – whether it is flame-resistant.

Consider the "feel" you want to give a room and choose the fabrics accordingly. If you want a rather grand and formal treatment, then velvets, silks, brocades and damasks will help to create the look. For a fresh, country scheme, on the other hand, flower patterns and crisp chintzes would be better, or mini-print florals and checked gingham.

If you want a definite period flavour, there are ranges of authentic designs available from some manufacturers, some of which may have been re-coloured to suit today's furnishing trends. For a feminine bedroom, lace, satins, or *broderie anglaise* would be an interesting choice. In a modern setting, crisp geometric prints on cotton, striped ticking, open-weave sheers, closely woven canvas will all follow the theme.

▲ *Crisp cotton pleats well for curtain and pelmet.*

Practicalities

As always, the purpose and function of the room is also important. Bathroom and kitchen window treatments may have to cope with grease and steam, while curtains, cushions and covers in family living rooms and children's rooms will need to be laundered fairly frequently. Bedroom fabrics can usually be more fragile.

If the window is exposed to strong sunlight for a large part of the day you should choose fade-proof fabrics, avoid strong or bright colours and don't use silk – even if carefully lined and interlined it tends to rot in sunlight. If you live on a busy roadway use textiles which are thick and grime/noise-absorbing, but also are easy to clean – and use lining and interlining for window treatments in such rooms.

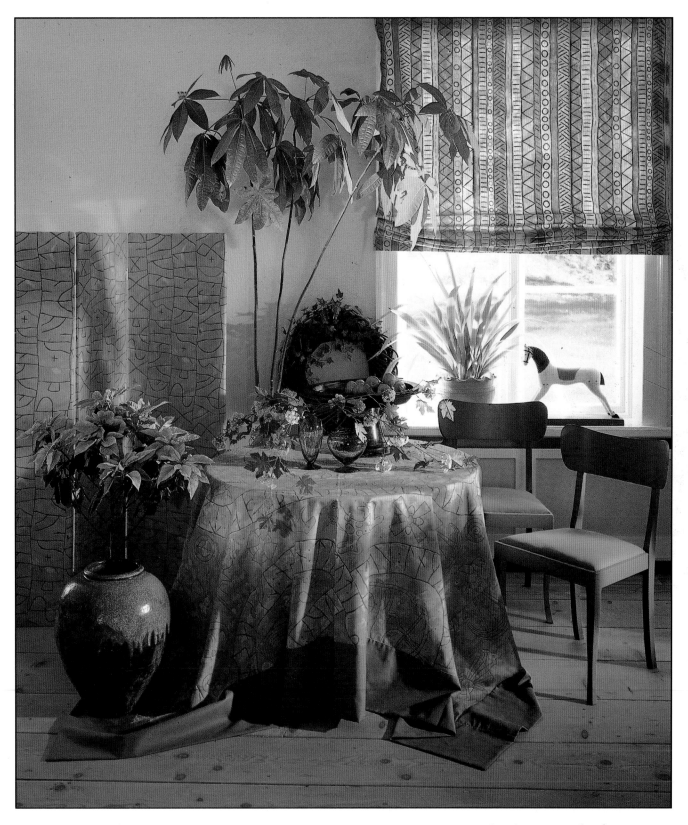

▲ *Strong designs scaled to suit the surfaces harmonise rather than overpower.*

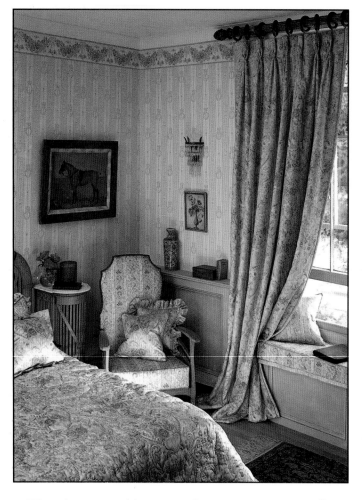

▲ *When choosing one fabric to co-ordinate a room, ensure it will be suitable for all uses.*

▲ *Perfectly co-ordinated pattern and plain fabrics on bed, cushion, windows . . .*

Fibres

The fibres used to make fabrics fall into three groups: natural (cotton, linen, silk, wool); man-made, which are natural fibres regenerated and chemically treated (rayon); and synthetic, which are completely chemically derived fibres (acetate, acrylic, nylon, Terylene, polyester etc.).

Fabrics made from natural fibres are generally dirt-resistant and clean well, but may shrink and crumple when cleaned. Materials from man-made fibres resist shrinkage and creasing and are less absorbent than natural cloths. Textiles made from synthetics attract dirt and need more frequent washing, which can spoil the texture. Many modern fabrics combine natural and man-made or synthetic fibres, thus giving the benefits of both.

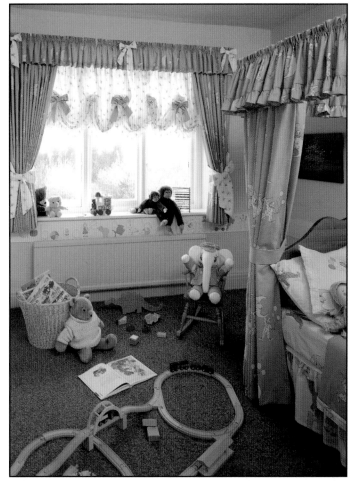

▲ *Mix and match contrasting fabrics with bow trimmings and tie-backs.*

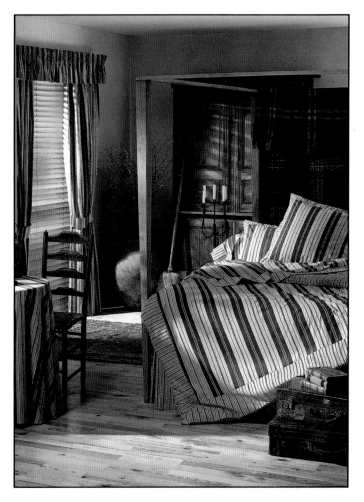

▲ *The lines of the slatted blinds are echoed by the striped fabric.*

Try before you buy

Once you have reached a decision, check the fabric for any flaws before you leave the shop. Ensure the grain of the fabric/printing is straight; if not, you will not be able to tear it along the grain, and may make mistakes when cutting lengths. Rub "budget" fabrics to see if a dressing has been applied to give extra body – this will come out at the first washing or cleaning, leaving the fabric limp and insubstantial. If the fabric is to be used for upholstery or loose covers ask about fire retardancy, and whether it is (or can be) treated to be stain resistant.

Always insist on buying fabric from the same roll to avoid any colour variation – if you have to order fabric, check that it comes from the same roll or batch number: the latter denotes the date of printing – if all the fabric comes from the same printing the colours should match.

CO-ORDINATION

SUCCESSFUL CO-ORDINATION can be tricky and if you are a little unsure of how to cope there are plenty of ready made co-ordinated or companion collections available which you can see – often in pattern book form – at local stockists.

These can include wallcoverings, borders and several different fabrics for curtains, upholstery, bed-linens and sheers. Some ranges even extend to waterproof fabric for shower curtains, ceramic tiles, flooring and accessories. The simpler companion collections have the same pattern printed on (or in some cases woven into) fabrics and wallcoverings. Others may have an identical design but in a different style, so that you can use a bold print at the window and a smaller version of the same pattern on the upholstery.

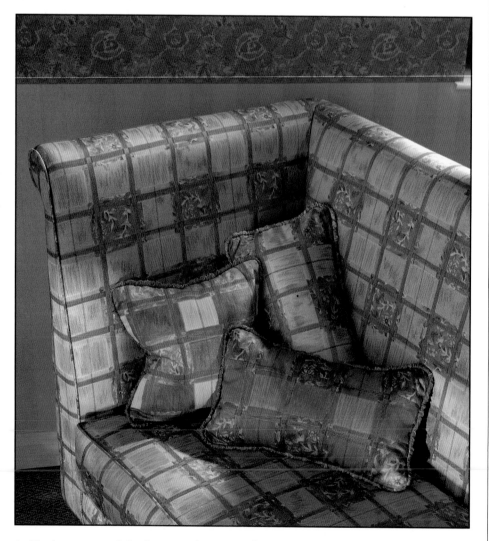

▲ *Checks, stripes and florals in co-ordinating mode.*

Pick and mix

But you need not be limited by ready made companion ranges; if you prefer, you can mix and match to suit your own taste. You could experiment with using several ranges from one manufacturer to achieve an original yet co-ordinated look, or select from several sources, since so many makers now work to a similar colour palette. Bear in mind, however, that this will only be effective if you choose a similar colour theme and similar motifs – for example, all florals, all geometric or all ethnic designs. These can be in a different scale, depending on the size of the area.

Cushions give you a good opportunity to start pattern mixing. Choose a fabric for the cushion to suit the basic shape – checks and stripes on a square, box or rectangular shaped cushion; florals for circular and heart-shaped ones – or be bold – try a check pattern on a heart-shaped cushion. Add a frill in a different pattern, coloured to co-ordinate. Try contrasting piping on a plain cushion to define the shape; trim with smart chequerboard braid – or lace and *broderie anglaise* if this suits the style. Pile cushions of different shapes, sizes and patterns on beds, sofas, chairs and window seats.

▲ *Mini-print patterns and lots of frills are teamed with plain walls.*

▲ *Well thought through co-ordination – the vase motif is highlighted on the cushions.*

▲ *Range of patterns all from the same colour palette.*

This approach can work well at the window too. A plain or striped valance could combine with floral-patterned curtains, or you could have a shaped plain pelmet above paisley-patterned curtains over a checked or striped Roman blind. Or a plain half curtain with an elaborate Austrian blind.

For the bedroom, reversible throw-over bedcovers or duvet covers and matching or contrasting pillowcases can complete the fully co-ordinated look, while matching placemats and napkins with a contrasting tablecloth make an ideal finishing touch in the dining room.

Personal touches

Co-ordinating or contrasting fabrics add a personal finishing touch which gives a scheme personality and individuality. If you have enough fabric make matching accessories such as cushions, napkins or tie-backs, or add a frill or covered buttons to an existing item.

Small pieces can be used for patchwork – if you are using old and new fabrics, try to combine like with like – a similar fibre, weight and texture, or there could be problems with shrinkage and puckering when the item is washed or cleaned.

A larger piece of leftover curtain fabric can be converted into a throw-over to hide a less-than-perfect cover on chair or sofa, or add

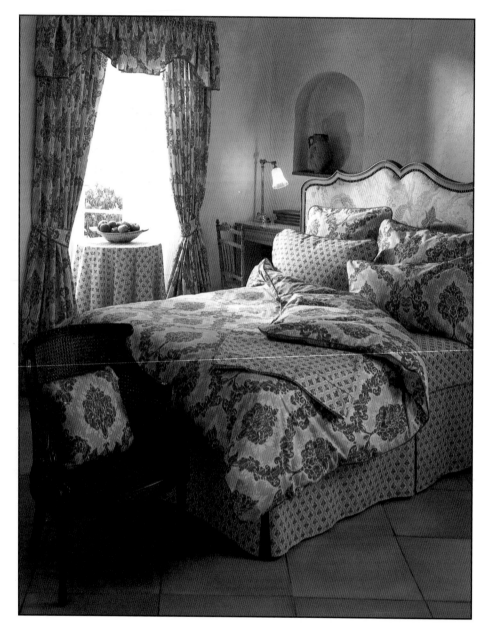

CO-ORDINATING TRIMS

• Ties in a matching or contrasting fabric make pretty fasteners for cushions or can be attached to curtains and tied to rods and poles for an attractive heading.

• Add a button covered in a co-ordinating fabric to a cushion or the base of each curtain heading pleats.

• Add contrasting tassels to each end of a bolster cushion or to the end of a plain tie-back.

◀ *Pillow cases, cushions, bolsters, duvet and co-ordinating valance link with frilled pelmet and tailored tie-backs.*

braid, lace, *broderie anglaise* or a frill as a trimming in keeping with the overall colour scheme. An even larger remnant can be used to "tie up" a small chair whose cover is past its prime, and wide sheeting or a large bedcover can similarly cheer up a tired sofa and co-ordinate with new curtains.

Matching or contrasting fabric can also be used to hide the plumbing under a bathroom or bedroom basin and transform it into a vanity unit. You can pleat and head the top to match existing or new curtains and

• Use matching or contrasting fabric to make ties for napkins instead of napkin rings.

• Add frills to placemats, cushions, pillowcases, blinds, tablecloths and tie-backs in a co-ordinating fabric to highlight a colour accent.

• Contrasting piping can be used to pick out a toning colour on cushions, pelmets and tie-backs.

use curtain track, or shirr onto a curtain wire held in place with hooks screwed to the wall, or use touch-and-close fastener. Dressing tables can be given a similar treatment.

Tailored Roman blinds in a dining area can be trimmed with braid to match the panelling on the door or shutters. And if your table is less than beautiful you could add a floor-length tablecloth in the same fabric with a contrasting or lace over-lay.

CURTAINS

The whole process of curtain making should be a pleasure from choosing the fabric to the final press, but because of the amount of fabric involved it can often be a daunting task. Following the guidance in this section, from the measuring of windows to the step-by-step instructions, will enable you to make professional-looking curtains for any room. There are simple unlined curtains made by machine, to lined, and interlined and lined curtains suitable for more expensive materials, as well as how to adapt "sheer" fabrics.

Seven steps to successful curtains

The following pages explain in detail the questions you should be asking yourself and the considerations you should ponder BEFORE buying fabric. This quick checklist emphasises the importance of the planning sequence that follows to ensuring that you will achieve results you will be happy to live with for many years.

1 THE ROOM

Curtains are just one item in a room. If you are lucky enough to be decorating the whole room from top to bottom then it is easier to achieve a truly stunning co-ordinated look. But, for most of us, it is a question of mixing and matching with what is already there.

Adding cushions and other accessories in the new curtain fabric can help pull a room together without costing a fortune.

Style
Do you want to change the style and feel of the room? Make it look warmer or cooler? Or are you happy with it as it is?

Enhance or Hide
Are there features in the room that can be brought out or hidden by new curtains?

Practicalities
Who will be using the room and when? Is it important to have easy-to-wash unlined curtains or thick interlined curtains to keep in warmth and keep out light? Are the radiators beneath the windows – in which case heat will be lost if you choose full length curtains.

2 THE WINDOWS

It is important to choose curtains that work well with the shape and size of your windows, both when the curtains are open and closed.

Size and Shape
Do you have differently or oddly shaped windows that need to be harmonised? Do you want to make a window look bigger, smaller, shorter or taller? Consider your choice of fabric and the positioning of tracks and poles.

Open and Shut
Will your choice of curtain and track make it difficult to open, close or clean windows or patio doors?

Light and Outlook
Do you want more light in a room for reading or studying? Do you want to block out the sun to avoid fading? Do you want to hide a really ugly view? Consider different types of curtains and/or blinds that will help with these problems.

3 CURTAIN ACCESSORIES

Assessing the style of your room and the shape of your windows inevitably extends your thoughts beyond a plain pair of curtains to tie-backs, valances, pelmets, swags and tails.

Decide Now
It is important to decide, before buying fittings or fabric, if you want any of these accessories as it will affect the type of track you buy and the amount of fabric you will need.

Inspiration
Take your time deciding. Look through this book, through magazines and in the homes of friends and neighbours while thinking if your own room will be enhanced by making the curtains more elaborate. It is worth thinking hard about as surprisingly little extra effort can turn a pair of home-made curtains into an interior designer's dream.

4
TRACK OR POLE?

It is best to choose your curtain track or pole and your curtain fabric at the same time as buying your curtain fabric to ensure the track is suitable to hold the weight of your chosen fabric and that the fitting and the fabric look good together. But DON'T BUY the fabric until the track or pole is fitted on to the wall or window. Only then can you take accurate measurements.

What Type?

A wide range of tracks and poles is now available. Look in local shops and browse through magazines for an idea of what's on the market before making expensive decisions. Consider the type of curtain the track or pole is for: sheer or net curtains; dress curtains; do you want to add a valance? Also, do you need to bend the track around curves or bays? Will the track show or be hidden by the style of curtain heading you choose? If it shows will you need to hide it with a valance or pelmet? Do you want corded tracks? What about poles?

Position with Care

You will need to decide on the position of the track or pole in relation to the window – for example, if you want to pull the curtains right back off the windows you will need extra length.

5
HEADINGS

Curtain fabric has to be attached to the curtain tracks or poles and this is usually done with heading tape. This tough tape is sewn to the top of the curtain and has pockets in it through which hooks can be slipped.

What Type?

There are many different kinds of heading tape available which give different effects. Consider one that will suit your overall chosen window style, from simple gathers to more formal goblet pleats.

Heading Tape

Your choice of heading tape affects the amount of fabric you will need to buy. More elaborate headings usually require more fabric.

Types Available

Standard gathered tape
Pencil pleat tape
Pinch pleat tape
Box pleat shape
Contact heading tape

6
MEASURING

Only when you have fixed the track or pole in position, chosen the style of heading tape and decided if you want any matching accessories can you measure accurately and calculate the amount of fabric needed.

Drop

To measure the drop or length of the curtain, measure from the point where the curtain will be suspended to your chosen length. Add allowances for top and bottom hems.

Width

To measure the width, measure the length of the track or pole, adding extra if you have an overlap arm.

Heading

Check the fullness of fabric needed for the heading of your choice and multiply by the track length.

Fabric

Now you must relate these length and width measurements to the width and pattern of the fabric of your choice.

7
BUYING FABRIC

Putting fabric last in this checklist doesn't mean that you shouldn't be thinking about fabric choices from the minute you decide to make new curtains. It just means that you shouldn't BUY any fabric until all the other considerations have been taken into account.

The best thing to do is to bring home swatches and samples of material while you ponder stages one to six. Look at the samples under different lights and at different times of day. Hold them against existing furnishings to judge the effect.

Cost

Big repeating patterns will probably require extra fabric to match the pattern when you join seams.

Colour, Texture and Pattern

Will they harmonise with existing furnishings and give the effect you want?

Practicalities

Will it wash if necessary? Will it need lining to keep out light or keep in warmth?

Extra Fabric

For matching or contrasting accessories like tie-backs and valances and for additional items such as cushions, bed linen etc.

MAKING ASSESSMENTS

WHATEVER THE STYLE of home, windows are a natural focal point in a room, and every window has exciting decorative potential. The way you dress your windows is more than just a question of choosing a fabric in keeping with other furnishings in the room and hanging a straightforward pair of curtains. The right treatment can dramatically improve or alter the appearance of even the most uninspiring window and bring character and distinction to the interior of any room.

Curtains are the natural choice for window dressing. Not only do they provide pattern, colour and texture; their value in practical terms cannot be ignored. They provide privacy, and a screen to blot out a grim view if necessary; they can be made so that they block outside light completely or let controlled amounts in; and above all, well-lined curtains are a helpful means of insulation – keeping the warmth in and the draughts out. Well-chosen curtains can enhance a feature window or dress up a dull one, and they can visually improve the proportions of an odd-shaped room and transform the outward appearance of the most drab exterior.

Of course, there are no hard and fast rules; it's your own personal taste that counts in the final analysis. But don't be rushed into making a decision you may come to regret – remember that fashions come and go, in home furnishings as in anything else, and your final choice is one you are likely to live with for a long time.

▲ *The tie-backs, pelmet and co-ordinated fabric make the window an attractive focal point.*

Choosing a style

Because curtains can make such an impact on a room, it's vitally important to choose the right style to suit the situation. There is a wide variety of treatments to choose from, but both the style and the fabric should always relate to the size, shape and architectural style of the window.

For example, large windows which dominate a whole wall in an elegant town house demand a lavish dressing with luxurious folds of fabric and decorative headings, but this grand approach would be quite wrong for small cottage-style windows. These need a simple uncluttered treatment, in crisp country cottons, scaled down to suit an altogether different environment.

Likewise, the window dressing should take into account the way in which the room is used and by whom. Fancy frilled curtains which might be out of place in a study or in a boy's bedroom could be just right for a feminine style bathroom. Expensive fabrics draped extravagantly to the floor might be the perfect touch in a single person's dream home, but could quickly become a nightmare in the family living room.

Practical considerations

Other constraints are often imposed by existing features in the room, a common problem being radiators beneath windows. Here too, personal choice is involved. While it makes the most practical sense to have short curtains that don't restrict the flow of heat into the room, there is no reason why you should not have full-length ones if you wish. In this case, though, it would be best to stick to lighter, more open-weave fabrics and avoid interlining.

One factor that cannot be ignored, of course, is your budget – even when you make your own curtains you still have to pay for the fabric, the lining and the heading tape. As a general rule, most curtains require at least twice the width of a window in fullness, and it is very unwise to skimp on this, as it will only lead to disappointing results. If you need to economize, it's better to opt for a less expensive fabric rather than cutting down on quantity. Look out for bargains at sales time or checkout discontinued designs often sold more cheaply by specialist fabric shops. Or you might find that using a plain fabric instead of a patterned one works out cheaper, and you can then invest in more lavish trimmings to bring it into the "designer" class. Draped generously, the cheapest fabric – even lining material – can look good, especially when it has been enhanced with pelmets, valances, or even swags and tails.

▲ *Elaborate swags and tails give immediate impact to a window area.*

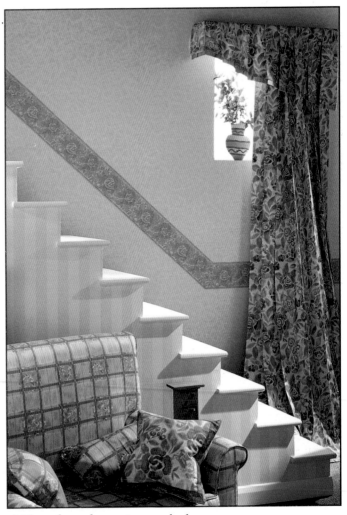

▲ *Floor draped curtains can look stunning but are not always practical.*

TYPES OF WINDOWS

WHETHER YOU ARE decorating a room from scratch or merely changing the curtains, it pays to take a completely fresh look at your windows, setting aside any preconceived ideas you may have. Sometimes the windows in a house are more or less uniform in size and shape, but often they are not. Where there are several differently shaped windows in the same room, think of the treatment as a whole so that you can create a unifying effect. For a window that is an attractive feature in its own right or looks out on a fine view, consider a treatment that makes the most of its good points. Alternatively, if the outlook is uninspiring and you need a screen from prying eyes, you'll need more than just a simple pair of curtains.

Bay windows

These are always a dominant feature, and curtains need careful planning to avoid costly mistakes. Before deciding on the width and length of the curtains, bear in mind that too much fabric will lead to unsightly bunching at the sides when the curtains are open, whereas too little will look skimpy.

Tall bay windows can take individual pairs of full-length curtains, tied back between the windows and linked with a continuous pelmet. When the curtains are drawn open, the pair either side of the central window will make elegant columns of fabric, which will define the angles of the bay.

Where the bay is small or bow-shaped, however, you can treat the window as a single unit, with one pair of curtains, each drawn well back at either side. A way of cutting the cost of curtaining a bay window is to have single-width dress curtains (those that are permanently tied back) only at the sides, using blinds for each window section to screen them at night.

Picture windows

Horizontal windows

Casement windows

Patio doors and large picture windows, with their vast expanse of glass, can look and feel cold at times, as well as being distinctly bleak at night. Lined and interlined curtains will help with the cold problem, and if they are hung full-length to cover the whole wall they will make a dramatic focus for the eye. Hang the curtains on a decorative pole or track, allowing sufficient length for them to be drawn well clear without affecting the opening of the doors. With such a large expanse of fabric, a heavyweight track with a cording mechanism is essential to maintain and protect the appearance of your curtains.

Typical of modern houses, these short, wide windows can be improved with clever dressing to lift them out of the ordinary. Careful positioning of the track or pole, which might be placed higher than usual, can help to correct unsatisfactory proportions. The fabric should be used generously, and preferably full length, except where there is a deep sill or radiator beneath.

These windows are sometimes placed too high to reach easily, in which case permanently fixed sheer curtains are often the only solution. Alternatively, if you must have curtains that open, use a track with a cording mechanism, and leave the cords extra long so they can be operated from ground level and wound round a cleat when the curtains are drawn back.

These double windows, usually opening outwards and hinged at both sides, are common to many older houses. If they are deepset, curtains can be mounted on track fixed inside the recess. However, if you prefer floor-length curtains, or those that hang just below the sill, you can fix the track or pole on the wall above the window.

Casement windows are sometimes arranged in groups of two, three or four, in which case the track or pole can run right along the length.

◄ *An unused patio door lends itself to a wide variety of window treatments that might not be possible with a door that's in constant use.*

Pairs of windows

Whatever form these take – they
may be a well-proportioned pair
side by side, or they may be
unevenly sized, or perhaps even
placed either side of a corner – they
are generally best dealt with as a
single unit.

Uneven and corner pairs

When adjacent windows differ in
size, you can fool the eye by
treating them as one. Hang the
track or pole across both windows
at the highest point, and use full-
length curtains to compensate for
the irregularities in the depth of the
windows.

Two windows placed either side
of a corner with little space in
between can make an eye-catching
feature when treated as a single
unit. In this case you will need
either to use a curtain track which
is sufficiently flexible to curve into
the corner angle or fix a pair of
poles, mitred at right angles and
with supporting brackets either side
of the join as well as at either end.

Identical pairs

Dormer windows

Skylights

The ideal treatment for two equal-sized windows positioned close together on a wall is a pair of full-length curtains headed with a deep valance or pelmet. If the windows fall short, hang the pelmet board well above the window to give an illusion of height; if they are narrow, extend the length of the track so that the drawn curtains cover the walls at the sides rather than the windows themselves.

For pairs of matching windows with a wide gap in between, you can introduce a sense of uniformity by having a third curtain to cover the space during the day. By night, the central curtain can be drawn in both directions to meet the pair at either side, making a feature of a generous expanse of draped fabric.

◀Provide balance and harmony between two identical windows by emphasizing the wall space between them.

Fixed into an extension projecting from the roof, dormer windows need special treatment, as there is rarely enough room on either side to hang conventionally drawn curtains. One solution is to attach a single curtain to the actual frame so that it remains in position when the window is opened. The fabric should obviously be sufficiently sheer to let in the light, and is made up with cased headings so that the curtain can be suspended from wires stretched across the top and bottom of the frame. Or, use contact tape with the "hook" side attached to the window frame.

Where the dormer recess is especially deep, and the window opens outwards, the curtain can be hung from a hinged rod. This will enable it to lie flat against the side wall during the daytime and to be swung inwards at night to cover the window. As both sides of the curtain will be visible, you will need to double the amount of fabric and conceal all seams to make it completely reversible.

Many windows at the upper level of the house, or possibly in a new extension, are set into the roof or high up a wall, and they also slope, which adds to the problem of choosing a suitable curtain treatment. One solution is to filter the light rather than blotting it out completely by mounting lightweight or sheer curtains directly to the frame on rods, wires or loop contact tape and hook tape at the top and bottom, as recommended for dormer windows. In some situations, it may be possible to hang full-length curtains from a pole fixed to the ceiling above the window and anchor them in place with a second pole set below the window in the angle where the ceiling and the wall meet.

Sash windows

Georgian-style sash windows are attractive in their own right, and call out for a curtain treatment that enhances their elegant proportions. Floor-length curtains look best, mounted outside and above the frame either on tracks or poles, but where there is a deep sill or a radiator beneath, short curtains may be your only option.

▶ *Floor-length curtains are ideal for sash windows and add colour to plain walls.*

Arched and round windows

Curtains for arched windows should be designed to emphasize their handsome outline, not disguise it. The simplest option is to hang sill- or floor-length curtains conventionally from a track or pole which is both long enough and high enough to prevent the drawn curtains from obscuring the frame in any way.

▶ *Round windows can be stylishly framed with curtains and pelmets.*

Doors and windows

Another potential problem is a glazed door flanked by a pair of small windows. The solution is to hang floor-to-ceiling curtains from an extended length of track so they can be drawn well away to the sides during the day without affecting the opening and closing of the door. If the track is positioned high enough you could add a plain or frilled valance along the whole length for a more co-ordinated look.

TRACKS AND POLES

BY THE TIME you have settled on a suitable style for your curtains, you will also have formed an idea of the method by which to hang them. Though the basic choice is between a track or pole, there are so many variations of both that it is worth spending a little time researching the wide range of options before making up your mind.

Perhaps the most important consideration is whether the type you choose will be strong enough to support the weight of the curtains – many manufacturers produce booklets to advise you and it makes sense to study these for guidance. Specialist shops and many department stores stock a full – and constantly updated – range of tracks, poles and accessories and should have trained members of staff only too willing to share their expertise with you. If they don't, shop elsewhere!

Your preference for a curtain track or pole will largely be determined by the overall appearance of the room. Poles are decorative features in themselves, whereas many curtain tracks are designed to blend insignificantly into the background. For decorative accessories, such as pelmets and valances, you will need to use tracks. A pole is ideal if you prefer the more informal appearance that can be achieved with a swag, when a length of fabric is swathed loosely around it.

In the past, the objection to using a pole was that the curtains could be difficult to draw, especially at tall windows. However, the introduction of poles with runners and a concealed drawing mechanism has considerably increased their efficiency as well as their decorative potential.

CURTAIN TRACKS

IF YOU THINK how often your curtains will be opened and closed during their life span, you will realize how important it is to buy well-made tracks and fittings that will guarantee their smooth running. Most tracks are now made from lightweight, pliable plastic, are cheap to buy and quiet to use, and there are different types suitable for any style of window dressing. "Multi-purpose" tracks are available, but generally it is better to choose a track specifically

designed to take the treatment you have in mind. A basic, inexpensive track is fine for unlined and simple lined curtains, but for large windows and heavy curtains, you will need a sturdier plastic or metal track.

Tracks are usually sold in a standard range of lengths, which can be cut to size, but it is also possible to buy a telescopic type, that allows the track to be adjusted exactly to size as it is being fitted. Most curtain tracks are sold in a kit

with all the fittings included, but, if you need to buy them separately, you will generally need one hook and runner per 10 cm (4 in) curtain width, plus one extra for the edge.

As the main purpose of the track is to give support, equal attention should be given to the fixing method – some are easier to install than others, but all come complete with full installation instructions. Most, but not all, tracks can be either wall- or ceiling-mounted – check before you buy.

The main types are:
Tracks with gliders

Tracks with gliders (or runners), which slot into grooves on the back of the track, are the ones most generally used for most styles of draw curtains.

◀ *Perfect for swags, café curtains and dress curtains, poles come in all shapes and sizes. Choose one that co-ordinates with the colours of the curtain fabric and with finials that reflect the overall style of the room.*

Invisible track

Ultra-slim curtain tracks, sometimes called pelmet tracks, are used in situations where you require the track to be as inconspicuous as possible – perhaps where it is fitted to the underside of a window frame. Suitable for lightweight curtains, they can be wall or ceiling mounted and can be curved around a bay.

Visible track

If the track will be in view, that is, not covered with a pelmet or valance, choose one that is unobtrusive or can be decorated to match your room scheme, either with paint, wallpaper or fabric. Alternatively, choose a decorative track, say with gold, silver or brass finish, complete with matching finials that fits in with your style of curtaining and complements your decor.

Bay window track

Cording and overlaps

Double valance tracks

For bay windows, you will need a track that is sufficiently pliable to be bent to fit around the curve and this is possible with most plastic tracks. If the track is warm it will be easier to bend, so it is helpful to have it at room temperature before you start. However, some are slightly more rigid than others and cannot, therefore, be curved as tightly, so may not be suitable for a right angled bay – check the manufacturer's literature for guidance on the most suitable choice.

For long and very heavy curtains, you will need a metal track that is strong enough to take their weight. Most metal tracks available can also be bent by hand, but a few – generally those used by professional designers – have to be 'made to measure' by the retailer.

When you are drawing a wide expanse of fabric across a bay or other large window, or where curtains are difficult to reach, it makes sense to invest in a track with an integral cording system. Supplied ready-assembled, with all the cords in position, and overlap arms where the curtains meet in the centre of the window, these tracks help to improve their "hang", maintain their shape and protect them from everyday wear and tear. As the curtains overlap, rather than butt together, it is important to allow for a little extra width in your calculations for fabric.

Though these tracks are more expensive, it is worth the extra cost, especially for delicate or pile fabrics which would be damaged with constant handling. However, certain corded tracks are only suitable for straight runs – remember to check before you buy.

It is possible to buy a cording set for an existing track, which includes clip-on overlap arms, but these are generally less efficient than the ready-corded type.

With the revival of the valance as a decorative top treatment for curtains, double tracks with combined valance rails are now widely available. The rail is attached to the track with extension brackets and comes with clip on hooks which allow the valance to be held firmly in place, but also easy to remove for cleaning. You can, of course, keep an existing track and suspend a shelf above it to take the valance – and this is the only method suitable for supporting a more rigid pelmet.

▶ For a bay window choose a pliable curtain track that bends to fit the curve.
▶ For a recessed window (far right), a fixed curtain on either side within the recess eliminates the need for a pliable track.

Net curtain tracks

For sheer or net curtains on their own, you can choose from the basic coated sprung wire, special lightweight track or slimline tension rods which carry net curtains neatly without the need for supporting brackets; used within a window frame, they spring out to grip the sides.

Multi-layered tracks

If you are considering a 'multi-layered' window treatment, with curtains, valance and sheers, for example, it is possible to buy a three- or four-tier system which has separate tracks for each one combined within the one unit.

Curtain draw rods

In the absence of a cording set, an alternative is to attach draw rods or pull rods to the lead runners at the centre of the window and use these to draw the curtains. Made from wood or metal, the rods are hidden behind the edge of the curtain.

CURTAIN POLES

WHERE A CURTAIN pole is more appropriate for your style of decor, there is a wide range of sizes and styles to choose from. They are available in either a wood – natural, stained, polished or painted – or metal finish, such as brass, iron and steel, and are usually supplied with wall mounting brackets and an appropriate number of rings for the length purchased. (For curtains with a cased heading, or rod pocket, you will obviously have no need for the rings). Finials complete the decorative effect of curtain poles – designs range from simple round knobs to fancy acorns, pineapples and fleurs de lys.

Standard curtain pole brackets allow the curtains to project up to 9 cm (3½ in) from the wall, a useful factor where clearance is needed for a radiator or window sill. However, short reach brackets are also available, as are recess brackets, which allow a pole to be suspended within a window frame, without finials. It is vital to use the right number of brackets for the length of pole – too few and you run the risk of it bending beneath the weight of the curtains.

Standard poles

Poles are available in a variety of widths – the choice of diameter ranges between 25 mm (1 in) and 35 mm (1⅜ in), and should be governed by the weight of the curtains the pole has to support. A range of lengths is also available – if you cannot find the precise size you require, all except solid brass poles can be cut to length and some incorporate a telescopic mechanism that allows the pole to be adjusted exactly to size as it is being fitted.

Poles are no longer limited to straight runs alone, as it is possible to buy corner connections to bring together two poles for curtaining windows either side of a corner.

Mini poles

Designed specifically for café curtains, mini "café rods" have a diameter between 12 mm (½ in) and 19 mm (¾ in). Sold in either brass or polished wood, these come with rings or clips which grip the top of the curtain, eliminating the need for curtain hooks.

Rod pocket poles

Standard poles can be used for curtaining with tunnelled or pocket headings, where the fabric is simply fed along the pole to create a ruched effect. In this way you can create elegant valances, static curtains, even swags and tails, both quickly and easily.

Corded poles

Where it is important to have a corded mechanism for drawing your curtains, corded poles have a similar appearance to the traditional style, but are fitted with half-rings – for decorative purposes only – and runners concealed at the back. As these tracks are extendable, they offer greater scope for hanging a particularly wide expanse of curtaining.

Corded poles can be used in conjunction with curtain tracks when a multi-layer effect is required.

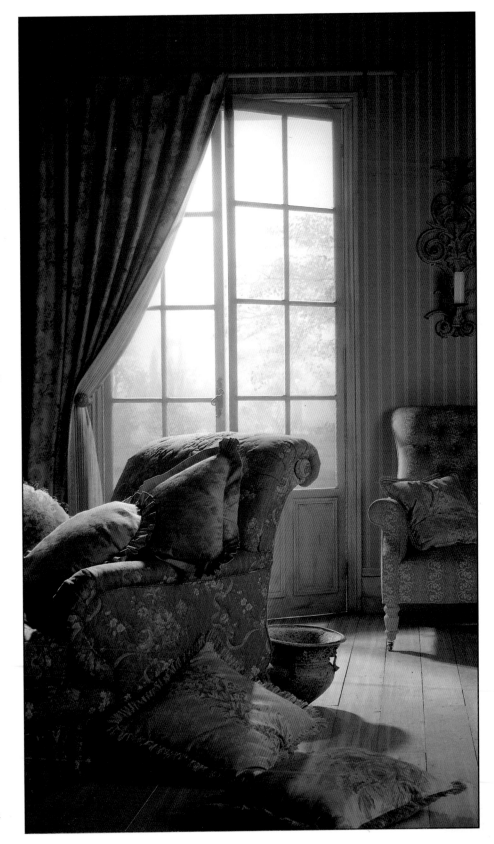

▶ *Match a curtain with a loop heading to a pole that co-ordinates with the wallpaper and contrasts with the curtain fabric.*

POSITIONING

WHEN BUYING a pole or track, remember to allow for the extra length required to enable curtains to be drawn back well away from the sides of the window and let in the maximum daylight. The distance will depend on the fullness and fabric used, but, if possible, tracks and poles need to extend beyond the window's edge by between 20 cm and 45 cm (8 in and 18 in).

When deciding where to position the track, bear in mind the points made in Making Assessments – if it is desirable to improve proportions, for example, raising or lowering the height of the track can considerably affect the appearance of a window that is either too short or too tall.

The fixture should be in position before starting to measure for your fabric.

Wall above window

The most usual position for fixing the curtain track or pole is on the wall above the window, and the ease with which this can be done depends on whether or not there is a concrete lintel above the window which would be difficult to penetrate. One solution is to put up a wooden batten to take the fixture, but remember it will project out slightly and will be visible when the curtains are open. If you're using a track, it is possible to fix a screw eye into the end of the batten close to the wall, so that you can attach the last curtain hook to it, thus concealing the "return".

Window meets ceiling

Where the top of the window meets the ceiling, you have no option but to use curtain track that is suitable for "top-fixing", or a pole with specially adapted brackets that enable it to be fixed to the ceiling. Take extra care when securing the fixture to the ceiling, especially where heavy-weight curtains are involved. It is essential the screws are either inserted directly into the joists, with plasterboard plugs, or into timber beams if you live in a modern timber-framed house.

FIXING THE TRACK OR POLE
The actual fixing for your chosen track or pole will vary from one manufacturer to another, so you should follow the instructions that accompany the fixture you have bought.

Recessed window

Where a window has a deep recess, you may choose to mount a top-fixed track, or a pole with recess brackets inside it. Here, too, you may come up against the problem of drilling into concrete and would, therefore, have to resort to fixing a batten.

Window frame

For curtains which need to lie close to the window, sheers for example, a lightweight fixture can be safely attached to the frame itself but with all other tracks, this position is not recommended as you run the risk of damaging the wood with the fixing screws.

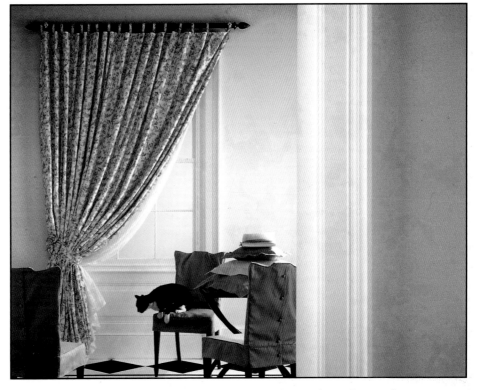

▲ *Poles are stylish heading features for curtains hung above the window.*

▲ *Curtains hung from the ceiling make the ultimate frame for a window.*

HEADINGS

BEFORE ESTIMATING and buying your curtain fabric, you need to decide on the heading style – there is now a wide variety of commercial tapes available, producing decorative effects that range from simple gathers to formal box pleats, even smocking. Your choice will depend on the effect you want to achieve and, to some extent, your budget. Some curtain heading tapes require more fullness of fabric than others, and it is, therefore, vital to choose your heading tape before buying your curtain fabric.

Standard curtain heading tapes are narrow strips of tough fabric, generally in white or cream, and sold by the metre. They have pockets for the curtain hooks which attach the curtains to the gliders on the track, making them easy to remove for washing or dry cleaning. For fixed curtains and valances, there are "contact" tapes, which work on the "touch-and-close" principle and require no hooks or rings.

With most heading tapes, drawstrings running through the tape enable gathers or pleats to be formed automatically as they are pulled up to the fullness required. Alternatively, there is a special tape for pinch pleats, where hooks, rather than drawstrings, are used to produce a crisp professional-looking heading.

Some of the deeper heading tapes have more than one row of pockets, enabling you to adjust the height of the curtain, according to which row you use for the hooks. With a pole the top row of pockets would be used for the hooks, to allow it to be seen, whereas with a track, the hooks are slotted into the bottom row to hide the track when the curtains are closed.

Before estimating your fabric needs, it is necessary to decide which row of pockets will be used for the hooks and include this in your calculations. The top hem allowance will be greater if you are using the bottom row of pockets, less if you use the top row. The depth of heading above the hook pocket plus a turning allowance at the top is needed.

Most curtain fabric suppliers should have a wide range of heading tapes to choose from, and also be able to offer you advice and a selection of leaflets produced by different manufacturers giving helpful guidance on using their own specific products. Be sure to refer to these before proceeding to calculate the amount of fabric required.

◀ *Buttons covered in a co-ordinating or matching material add an eye-catching detail to many items and can be stitched to the bottom of goblet and other pleats for that special touch.*

Standard gathered tape

Suitable for use with lightweight curtains hanging from a track, or those where the heading will be hidden by a valance or pelmet, the cheapest standard tape is approximately 2.5 cm (1 in) wide. It is generally positioned with a narrow margin of fabric between the top of the tape and the top of the curtain to form a neat frill when the cords are pulled up. Where a wider frill is required, the use of iron-on stiffening will prevent it from flopping forwards, and this is also a good idea to give a little extra body to the heading of sheer fabrics.

- Hook pocket rows: 1
- Fabric fullness required:
$1\frac{1}{2}$ to $2 \times$ the track length
- Clearance from top of tape to top of curtain: 2.5 cm (1 in)

◀ *Elegant triple pleat heading with pole and rings.*

Pencil pleat tape

A versatile heading, which suits most types of curtains, pencil pleat tape is available in a variety of widths and produces uniform, evenly spaced pleats when the cords are drawn up. Standard pencil pleat tape can be used with any type of track or pole; the fabric fullness required will depend on the type of fabric used – the thinner the fabric, the more fullness is needed. There is also a mini pencil pleat tape suitable for lightweight fabrics and a special one for sheers.

- Hook pocket rows: 2 (standard); 1 (mini)
- Fabric fullness required:
$2\frac{1}{4}$ to $2\frac{1}{2} \times$ the track length
- Clearance from top of tape to top of curtain: 3 mm ($\frac{1}{8}$ in)

Triple or pinch pleat tape

This type of heading produces regular groups of fanned pleats with spaces in between. The pleats are formed automatically by pulling up the cords and inserting special hooks to hold them firmly in place. Stiffer than some tapes, it creates a tall and elegant heading that is particularly attractive with formal lined curtains, and is equally suited to cottons and medium- to heavyweight fabrics.

As the pleat and space positions are pre-determined and cannot be altered, careful placing of the tape is necessary to ensure the heading matches across the curtains to give a continuous effect when they are drawn. Where a pair of curtains will butt together, always begin by placing the heading tape to the curtain edge which will lie in the centre of the window, starting in the middle of a pleat group, so you will be left with a half space at each edge. With an overlap arm, one complete space on each curtain should be adequate.

- Hook pocket rows: 2
- Fabric fullness required:
$2 \times$ the track length
- Clearance from top of tape to top of curtain: 3 mm ($\frac{1}{8}$ in)

Box pleat tape

Suitable for all types of curtains, particularly heavy, lined ones, box pleat tape pulls up the fabric into regular neat folds. It is well suited to permanently fixed dress curtains or those teamed with a valance – the top row of hook pockets could be used for the valance, the bottom row for the curtains.
- Hook pocket rows: 2
- Fabric fullness required: 3 × the track length
- Clearance from top of tape to top of curtain: 3 mm ($\frac{1}{8}$ in)

Uncorded triple pleat tape

A deep heading tape with long narrow pockets running at regular intervals along the full depth, with an opening at the bottom. Instead of drawstrings, long-pronged pleater hooks are used to draw up the pleats – by inserting the prongs into the pockets, you can make single, double or triple pleats. With this tape, your curtain can be "tailor-made" to the exact length of your particular fixture, as you can adjust the amount of fabric in each pleat and the spaces in between.

When using this tape, it is important to work out the approximate width down to which the fabric will pleat, and you should follow the manufacturer's instructions for guidance. A good tip is to pleat up the tape before applying it to the curtain, and hook it on to the track or pole to judge the effect. Place the first hook to make a single pleat at each end of the curtain and space the remainder evenly across the width, keeping the design continuous at the centre of a pair (see above).
- No. of pockets: (see above)
- Fabric fullness required: $2\frac{1}{4}$ to $2\frac{1}{2}$ × the track length
- Clearance from top of tape to top of curtain: 3 mm ($\frac{1}{8}$ in)

Cartridge or goblet pleat tape

A deep – up to 9 cm ($3\frac{1}{2}$ in) – tape which produces cylindrical tubes when drawn up and is especially suitable for heavy, lined, floor-length curtains. As the curtains fall in regular folds, rather than gathers, it is a good choice where a valance is being used. Special hooks secure the pleats firmly in position and the addition of a little wadding or tissue in the opening in the pleats enhances their firm rounded shape.

Goblet-shaped pleats can be made using the same tape (though a special goblet pleat tape is now available), but by pinching in each pleat at its base with a few hand stitches.
- Hook pocket rows: 2
- Fabric fullness required: 2 × the track length
- Clearance from top of tape to top of curtain: 3 mm ($\frac{1}{8}$ in)

Contact heading tape

Heading tapes with a contact backing can be used for simpler fixing of gathered valances, lightweight sheers and curtains at unusually shaped windows. Similar in appearance to conventional tape, with cords which pull up to form the gathers in the normal way, they have a "loop" backing which will adhere to a 'hook' tape fixed to the curtain track, batten or, in the case of sheers, the window frame. The hook side of these tapes is self-adhesive.
• Fabric fullness required: 2 to 3 × the track length (depending on tape used and application)
• Clearance from top of tape to top of curtain: 3 mm ($\frac{1}{8}$ in)

▶ Attractive rod pocket headings are easy to make and are perfect for dress curtains that remain in a fixed position.

Rod pocket heading

One of the simplest curtain headings requires no tape, hooks or rings – a casing or "pocket" is stitched through a double thickness of fabric below the top of the curtain, and a rod, pole or wire is inserted into it. The fabric fullness is then gathered up, creating a frill above it, if required. The fullness needed for this type of heading will vary considerably according to the weight of fabric – the thinner the fabric, the greater the fullness of the finished curtain.

Curtains finished in this way cannot be drawn, but they can be looped back attractively on either side of the window with matching tie-backs, or draped over brass or wooden hold-backs screwed to the window frame. This is an ideal heading for valances which always remain permanently fixed in place.
• Fabric fullness required: 1½ to 3 × the rod length (depending on the thickness of fabric)

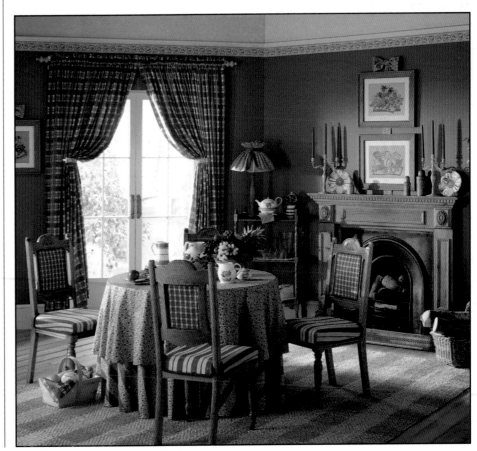

ATTACHING HEADING TAPE

WHEN YOU ARE ready to position your heading tape, refer to the manufacturer's instructions for the precise amount of fabric clearance between the top of the heading tape and the top of the curtain required for the particular type you are using. There may be some variation, ranging from a mere 3 mm ($\frac{1}{8}$ in) for deep heading tapes to 2.5 cm (1 in) or more, for standard gathered tape where a frill above it is required. Be sure to include any turning allowances when you are estimating fabric quantities.

1 Cut a length of heading tape to the width of the curtain, adding an allowance of 3 cm (1$\frac{1}{2}$ in) for the end turnings. If using drawstring tape, loosen the cords at the end of the tape which will come on the inside edge of the curtain, and knot each one on the wrong side, 1.5 cm ($\frac{5}{8}$ in) away from the cut edge. Leave the cords free for gathering at the outside edge by pulling them from the front of the tape and knotting the ends.

2 Turn under the 1.5 cm ($\frac{5}{8}$ in) allowance at each end and pin then tack the tape in place. Machine stitch first the top then the bottom edge of the tape, working in the same direction on each side to prevent puckering. Machine stitch across each end of the tape.

3 To gather a curtain with drawstring tape, hold the free cords in one hand and push the heading along the cords until the fabric is gathered to the width required. Distribute the fullness evenly along the curtain then knot the cords together at the outside edge. Insert hooks at approximately 8 cm (3 in) intervals along the curtain.

4 Do not cut loose cords of drawstring tape, so they can easily be released for washing or dry cleaning. Either thread them through the hooks at the back of the curtain for a short way, or wind them around a cord tidy, which can be hidden behind the outside edge of the curtain.

*Tracks, poles and heading tape
need to be carefully chosen to ensure
you achieve the effect you want.*

PLEATING

To pleat a curtain with drawstring tape, proceed as above, taking care to avoid puckering between pleats. Hold the top of the curtain firmly in one hand, with your thumb just in front of the first pleat group, and the loose cords in the other. Push the first pleat into position and then move on to the second. Now return to the first, as this will no longer be pleated and continue working forwards and backwards in this way along the curtain until the entire heading is pleated. Knot the cords and insert hooks, if using, into the two adjacent pockets at either side of a pleat to hold it firmly in place.

To pleat a curtain with uncorded tape, plan the position of the pleats, spacing them evenly along the curtain, and insert pleater hooks according to the manufacturer's instructions.

MEASURING THE FABRIC

ONCE YOU HAVE decided on a style of heading for your curtains and fixed the track or pole in its desired position, you are ready to estimate the amount of fabric required.

Only two measurements are necessary when making curtains – the drop for the finished curtain measured from the hook suspension point on the track and the length of the curtain track, plus overlap arm if the corded method of drawing is being used.

Use a steel decorator's tape or wooden metre/yardstick for accuracy and make a note of the appropriate measurements on a diagram of your window, as shown.

A true conversion from metric to imperial cannot always be made so work following one or the other throughout a project.

TO CALCULATE THE DROP

To calculate the finished drop of your curtains, first you need to decide where they will finish: to the sill, to just below the sill, or to the floor.

▲ **Sill length** curtains should actually end 1.5 cm to 2 cm (⅝ in to ¾ in) above a protruding sill to give clearance.

▲ **Below the sill** curtains should hang below the sill by 5 cm to 10 cm (2 in to 4 in). However if there is a radiator immediately below the window, end the curtains 1.5 cm to 2 cm (⅝ in to ¾ in) above it.

▲ **In a recess** curtains should end 1.5 cm to 2 cm (⅝ to ¾ in) above the sill to give clearance.

▲ **Floor length** curtains require a clearance of 2.5 cm (1 in) if you want to protect the hemline. However you may perhaps choose to make them over-long, so the fabric falls in swathes on the floor. If so, remember to adjust your measurements accordingly before starting to calculate for fabric requirements.

To measure the drop

Measure from the point where your curtain will be suspended to your chosen drop.

For a pole, this will be the finished drop measurement.

When using a track, rod or wire, you will need to add the additional depth of fabric from the suspension point to the top of the curtain.

Adding hems

To this finished drop measurement, you need to add the appropriate allowance for the hems at the top and bottom of the curtain, to give you the actual cutting length.

Bottom hem allowance

Unlined	8 cm (3 in)
Café curtains	not appropriate
Rod Pocket	8 cm (3 in)
Tube-lined	10 cm (4 in)
Locked-in lining	15 cm (6 in)
Locked-in lining and interlining	10 cm (4 in)
Detachable lining	not appropriate

Top hem allowance

The amount of extra fabric you need to allow for the top hem of your curtain depends on the type of heading tape you choose. For example: the top hem allowance for an unlined curtain using standard tape is 7.5 cm (3 in) to give a 2.5 cm (1 in) frill effect above the heading tape.

For the lined curtains, measure from the row of hook pockets being used to the top of the heading tape, then add the following measurements:

Café curtains	not appropriate
Rod pocket	check circumference of pole
Tube-lined	7.5 cm (3 in)
Locked-in lining	1.5 cm (⅝ in)
Locked-in lining and interlining	7.5 cm (3 in)
Detachable	not appropriate

TO MEASURE THE WIDTH

Once you have the drop measurement, calculate the width required. When you have these two measurements turn to the next page to estimate how much fabric you will need.

- Measure the length of your track or pole to calculate the width of the curtains when gathered. Add extra for an overlap arm and for the returns at the side.

- For curtains that will hang close to the window, measure the actual width of the recess.

TO ESTIMATE FABRIC

CHECK THE FULLNESS of fabric required for your chosen heading tape (see page 48). This can range from 1½ times to 3 times the actual length of your track or pole.

• Check the width that your chosen fabric is sold in.

• When working with patterned fabrics, especially where the design is large and distinct, think about where the hemline will fall, aiming to avoid an unsightly cut through a whole motif. Bearing in mind that the fullness of the curtain will obscure the pattern, consider the finished appearance at the top of the curtain, too, taking into account where the hooks will be placed in the heading tape for your chosen method of hanging.

• Remember, if you want to make co-ordinating items buy extra fabric when buying your main curtain fabric.

• See Working with Fabric, page 138.

• See Working with Fabric, page 138.

CUTTING TIPS FOR CURTAINS

• To prepare fabric for cutting, press out any creases. If there is a centre fold this will require a damp cloth and a warm/hot iron to press it out completely.

• Ideally a large table is best for preparing and cutting out fabric. If this is not possible, use the floor.

FOUR EASY STAGES

Multiply the track or pole length by the fullness needed for your chosen type of heading tape, then divide this figure by the width of the fabric, rounding up to the nearest whole number. This gives you the number of widths you will need.

↓

Usually the same track or pole will be carrying two curtains – one for each side, so you need to halve this amount to find out the number of widths in each curtain. If this means you have to divide widths in half, join the half widths to the outside edge of each curtain.

↓

Once you have established the total number of widths needed to cover the window, multiply this figure by the cutting length to give your total fabric requirement. It is advisable to allow a little extra fabric to enable you to straighten the cut edges, and to make any fine adjustments to the finished length.

↓

When using patterned fabric, you will need to make extra allowance for matching – as a general rule, allow one full pattern repeat for each width after the first. Any wasted fabric can be used to make tie-backs and matching cushions.

If the curtain drop takes in complete pattern repeats, as in A, there will be no wastage.

However, if partial repeats are required, as in B, there will be some wastage.

LINING

To calculate for plain fabric for curtains hanging outside the window and reaching the floor. The chosen fabric width is 137 cm (54 in) wide.

		cm	in
1	Measure track length (**A** to **B**)	127	50
	overlap arm	+15	6
	returns	+20	8
2	For pencil pleat heading tape, fabric required is 2.5 times the track length	=405	160
3	Divide this by fabric width, say 137 cm (54 in), (round up to the nearest full width)		
	widths	**3**	**3**

This will make two curtains with a width and a half each,

		cm	in
4	For length, measure **A** to **C**	215.5	85
5	Deduct for clearance	2.5	1
		=213	84
6	Add for hems and heading	2.5 cm	10 in
7	Multiply by required number of widths (3)	238	94
	Purchase:	**7.3 metres**	**8 yards**

This allows a little extra fabric to enable you to straighten the cut edges, and to make any fine adjustments to the finished length

GENERALLY, THE AMOUNT of lining required will be the same as the quantity of the curtain fabric and, as it is plain, you do not require extra for matching. But, as linings are made slightly smaller than the curtains, so you can purchase a little less for each drop required. The width is only reduced by trimming off a margin from the outer side edges, not from each width.

Tube-lined

Cut lining 15 cm (6 in) less each length.
Trim lining 5 cm (2 in) from each outer edge.

Locked-in lining

Cut lining 9 cm (3½ in) less each length.
Trim lining 4 cm (1½ in) from each outer edge.

Locked-in interlining and lining

Cut lining 10 cm (4 in) less each length.
Trim lining 5 cm (2 in) from each outer edge.
Cut interlining as the curtain, after joining widths minus all hems.

Detachable lining

Measure from bottom of existing heading tape to the hem. Deduct 2.5 cm (1 in) and add 8 cm (3 in). Lining can be same width as curtain or 1½ times the track.

DRAPING

Even the most professionally made curtains will not look their best unless they are draped correctly.

Hold the bottom hem at a position in line with the pleat at the top and gently tug at the hem. Now run your fingers down the length of the curtain along the naturally created folds.

If the curtains hang below the track, push each space between the pleats backwards whilst gently moving the curtains to the side of the window. If the curtain heading covers the track, the spaces between the pleats must be pulled forward, so they stand proud of the track. The draping should be held gently in position at intervals down the length of the curtain, using something soft, such as spare material. Leave at least overnight in order to "train" the pleats.

UNLINED CURTAINS

Unlined curtains are easy to make. They are best for a room such as kitchen or bathroom, where curtains need frequent laundering, and for windows where short curtains are required. Cotton or a polyester/cotton mix is best for a kitchen, and towelling for a bathroom as this withstands a steamy atmosphere.

1 Lay the fabric right side down and turn in each side edge 1.5 cm ($\frac{5}{8}$ in) to the wrong side. Pin near the cut edge, and press the folds. (If using towelling do not press.)

2 Turn in a further 1.5 cm ($\frac{5}{8}$ in) down each side to form double hems. Pin, tack, and remove the pins. Press the hems.

3 Machine stitch down each side hem. Remove the tacking and press the hems again. Turn up the bottom edge of the curtain 4 cm (1$\frac{1}{2}$ in) to the wrong side. Pin in place and press the fold.

4 Turn in a further 4 cm (1$\frac{1}{2}$ in) at the bottom edge of the curtain. Pin, tack and remove the pins. Press the hem.

5 Machine stitch the bottom hem. Remove tacking and press the bottom hem again.

6 Turn down the top edge 4 cm (1$\frac{1}{2}$ in) to the wrong side. Pin, tack and remove the pins. Press the hem. Attach the heading tape, and gather and hang the curtain.

CAFÉ CURTAINS

1 Cut a piece of fabric the width of the window plus 10 cm (4 in), by the drop length required plus 15 cm (6 in). Cut a strip 12.5 cm (5 in) wide and long enough to make sufficient loops. As a guide, one loop is placed at each end and then spaced approximately 10–15 cm (4–6 in) apart.

2 On the curtain piece make a hem, turning 1.5 cm ($\frac{5}{8}$ in) twice down the sides and hem the top and bottom, turning 5 cm (2 in) twice. Fold the loop strip in half lengthways with right sides facing and machine stitch 1.3 cm ($\frac{1}{2}$ in) from the raw edges. Press the seam open placing it in the centre of the strip.

3 Cut the loop strip into the desired lengths. Mark and stitch a point at one end of each piece. Trim excess fabric and turn right side out and press.

4 Place one loop at the end on the right side at the top of the curtain about 2.5 cm (1 in) down, bring the pointed end over to cover the raw edges. Tack and top stitch through all thicknesses. Position another loop at the other end of the curtain and space the remainder along evenly.

5 Thread the pole through the loops ready to hang at the window.

Unlined curtains are a quick and simple way to create a co-ordinated look in a bathroom, kitchen or children's room. Add tie or loop headings for instant visual impact.

TUBE-LINED CURTAINS

A lining protects the curtain fabric from the effects of sunlight and the dirt and dust from an open window. As tube-lining is done by machine it is a quick and easy method of lining curtains, and is ideal for a situation where the curtains may be changed frequently.

1 Stitch a line of tacking to mark the hem allowances 7.5 cm (3 in) from the top and 10 cm (4 in) from the bottom of the curtain fabric.

4 Place the lining right side down over the curtain, aligning the side edges and positioning the top and bottom of the lining 7.5 cm (3 in) from the cut edges of the curtain.

2 Lay the fabric right side down and turn in each side edge 3.5 cm (1⅜ in) to the wrong side. Pin near the cut edges and press the folds. Remove the pins.

5 Pin the lining to the curtain at the sides. Tack together and remove the pins.

3 Lay the curtain fabric right side up and open out the pressed sides. Make a lengthways fold in the fabric to take up the fullness as the curtain is wider than the lining.

6 Machine stitch the side seams 1 cm (⅜ in) from the raw edges, starting at the top and ending 20 cm (8 in) from the bottom edge.

7 Turn right side out and press the side edges again. Tack the lining to the top of the curtain along the marked hemline.

10 Form mitred corners at the bottom. Slipstitch the corners and the hem, and press.

8 Fold the top hem allowance over the top of the lining, pin and press the fold in place. Remove the pins. Attach the heading tape.

11 Turn up 2.5 cm (1 in) twice for a double hem at the bottom of the lining and pin in place. Tack, remove the pins, machine stitch the hem, and press.

9 Turn up the bottom of the curtain fabric by 5 cm (2 in) twice to make a double hem. Pin in place and press. Remove the pins.

12 Slipstitch the loose lining to the sides of the curtain, and slipstitch along the hem for 2.5 cm (1 in) from each side. Gather heading tape and hang the curtain.

A lined curtain but quickly made by machine, it is an ideal method for less expensive curtain fabrics. Add a lined valance to give a special touch.

LOCKED-IN LINING

Locked-in lining is done by hand and therefore takes a little bit longer, but it gives a better result, ensuring that the lining stays in place and hangs well with the curtain. This method is ideal for curtains that are expected to last a long time.

1 Lay the curtain fabric right side down and turn in each side edge 4 cm (1½ in) to the wrong side. Pin the sides near the cut edges and press the folds. Remove the pins.

2 Turn up 7.5 cm (3 in) twice across the bottom to form a double hem and pin in place. Press the hem and remove the pins.

3 Form mitred corners at the bottom. Slipstitch the corners and the hem. Sew the side hems using a medium to large herringbone stitch. Press the sides, and hem.

4 Mark the turning allowance at the top of the curtain with a line of tacking 1.5 cm (⅝ in) below the raw edge.

5 Mark vertical lines with tailor's chalk on the wrong side of the prepared curtain, ruling the first down the centre, then ruling further lines towards each side, spacing them about 30 cm (12 in) apart.

6 Turn up the bottom of the lining 5 cm (2 in) twice to form a double hem and pin in place. Machine stitch the hem and then press.

7 With right sides facing, fold the lining in half. Form a crease down the centre from top to bottom.

8 Lay the curtain fabric right side down and place the lining wrong side down over it. Position the lining hem 4 cm (1½ in) above the curtain hem and align the raw edges of the lining with the side and top edges, matching the crease line and the centre tailor's chalk line. Pin then tack the lining to the curtain.

9 Remove the pins. Fold back the lining. Work a loose lockstitch, starting 15 cm (6 in) from the top and ending 10 cm (4 in) from the bottom of the lining hem.

10 Lockstitch all the marked lines in the same way, working outwards from the centre line and alternating from side to side.

11 Smooth the lining towards the sides. Turn under the raw edges 2 cm (¾ in) and pin to the curtain side hems. Slipstitch the sides and along the hem for 4 cm (1½ in) from each side. Press the sides and hem.

12 Pin and tack the lining and curtain fabric together across the top. Turn down the marked allowance and tack it in place. Attach the heading tape, gather and hang the curtain.

A locked-in lining is sewn to the curtain fabric at regular intervals down the width by hand, which gives the curtains a professional finish and ensures smooth and easy draping. Add a personal touch with a co-ordinating tie-back.

LOCKED-IN INTERLINING

Curtains can be interlined by inserting a piece of thin wadding between curtain fabric and lining to provide extra insulation, reduce the amount of light filtering through, and help muffle outside noise. This method should be used with more expensive curtain fabrics as it gives a highly professional finish and helps to protect the curtain fabric from wear and tear.

1 Lay the curtain fabric right side down. Mark the turning allowances: 7.5 cm (3 in) from the top with a line of tacking, 5 cm (2 in) from the sides and 10 cm (4 in) from the bottom with tailor's chalk.

2 Mark a vertical line down the centre of the curtain fabric using tailor's chalk. Working out from the centre, mark lines 30 cm (12 in) apart out to the sides.

3 Place the interlining over the wrong side of the curtain fabric, with the cut edges against the marked turning allowances.

4 Fold back the interlining away from the centre line and pin the interlining and fabric together. Work a loose lockstitch down the line, starting and finishing 7.5 cm (3 in) from the edge of the interlining.

5 Lockstitch all vertical marked lines in the same way, working outwards from the centre line and alternating from side to side, smoothing the interlining between each row before pinning.

6 Fold the turning allowances of the curtain sides and bottom hem over the interlining, pin and press. Form a mitre at each bottom corner and slipstitch the mitred corners.

9 Fold the lining in half and pin it to the interlining down the centre 2.5 cm (1 in) from the previous line of stitching, starting and finishing 15 cm (6 in) from the top and bottom. Lockstitch the lining to the interlining 2.5 cm (1 in) away from the previously lockstitched lines. Remove the pins.

7 Herringbone stitch the sides and hem of the curtain to the interlining. Tack the curtain fabric and interlining together at the top.

10 Smooth the lining towards the sides, top and hem. Turn under the sides of the lining 2.5 cm (1 in) and the bottom 5 cm (2 in). Pin and then slipstitch to the sides and hem of the curtain. Remove the pins.

8 Place the lining wrong side down over the interlining, and align the raw edges with the edges of the interlined curtain.

11 Tack the lining and the curtain fabric together across the top. Turn down the marked allowance and pin in place. Press the fold and remove the pins. Attach the heading tape, gather and hang.

An interlined curtain is ideal for lounge or dining room curtains where a more luxurious fabric is being used. For a really glamorous look add matching or contrasting swags and tails.

DETACHABLE LINING

There are several advantages to detachable linings: they can be laundered separately, which is useful if they need frequent washing, they can be easily replaced and they can be used to line an existing unlined curtain. The linings do not necessarily have to be as wide as the curtain itself. They are made in the same way as unlined curtains, but with a different type of heading tape.

1 Lay the lining fabric right side down. Turn in each side edge 1.5 cm ($\frac{5}{8}$ in) twice to the wrong side and pin in place. Machine stitch the sides close to the inside fold, removing the pins as you stitch. Press the sides.

2 Turn up 4 cm ($1\frac{1}{2}$ in) twice to the wrong side at the bottom and pin in place. Machine stitch across the bottom close to the upper fold, removing the pins as you stitch. Press the hem.

3 Check that the lining will be 2.5 cm (1 in) shorter than the curtain, keeping in mind that no turning allowance is needed at the top.

4 Slot the raw edge of the lining between the two flaps of the detachable lining heading tape, allowing an extra 2.5 cm (1 in) of tape at each side.

5 Knot the cords together at the sides that will meet at the centre of the window.

6 Pin and tack the tape in place, removing the pins as you work, ensuring that the lining fabric is completely enclosed by the tape.

7 Fold each end of the tape over the side edge of the lining and stitch across the ends and along the lower edge of the tape. Remove the tacking and press the lining.

8 Pull up the free cords, gathering the lining until it is 5 cm (2 in) narrower than the curtain. Insert the hooks into the lining heading tape, then into the curtain tape, to attach the two layers together.

9 Attach the lining to the curtain at intervals down the sides, either with catchstitches, or by hand-sewing strips of touch-and-close fastener to the curtain and lining.

A detachable lining is quick and easy to make for an existing unlined curtain, a temporary curtain or for a curtain fabric that is dry clean only. Add a special touch with a quick swag in matching fabric.

SHEER CURTAINS

'Sheer' is a description given to very lightweight fabrics, they are translucent to varying degrees and range from muslin to lace. Generally, a fullness from two to three times the width of the window is required. You can buy sheer fabric to make your own curtains, see Method One, or you can adapt ready-to-hang curtains, see Method Two. Methods Three and Four use fabric with finished side edges some of which has an extra detachable border edge used to trim the bottom hem.

CHECKLIST

Materials

fabric	page 54
heading tape (optional)	page 48
general sewing equipment	page 134

Techniques

French seam	page 143
machine stitching	page 140

Method One

1 Cut the fabric into drop lengths and trim off the selvedge. Join lengths with French seams if necessary to get the required width.

2 Turn in 1 cm (⅜ in) twice to the wrong side to make a double hem down each side and pin in place. Machine stitch the hems and remove the pins as you stitch.

3 Turn up 2.5 cm (1 in) twice to the wrong side to form a double hem at the bottom and pin in place. Machine stitch the hem and remove the pins as you cutch.

4 Make the casing at the top by turning under 1 cm (⅜ in) and pin in place. Press the fold and remove the pins.

5 Turn down a further 4 cm (1½ in) and pin in place. Press the fold and machine stitch close to the bottom edge of the hem removing the pins as you stitch.

6 Work another row of machining 1 cm (⅜ in) from the top edge. Thread the wire or rod through the channel between the two rows of stitching.

Method Two

1 Before making the side hems you need to unpick the applied heading for 2.5 cm (1 in) on each side. Follow Step 2, Method One to form double hems down each side.

2 Trim off 1 cm (⅜ in) from each side of the heading, turn under 1 cm (⅜ in) to neaten, and machine back in place.

Method Three

To shorten this type of curtain fabric, unpick and take off the heading. Trim off from the top edge to give the correct drop measurement. Make the side hems and reapply the heading, neatening the ends as in steps above.

Method Four

1 Make the casing across the top following steps 4, 5 and 6 as Method One.

2 Make a double bottom hem as shown in step 3 Method One, *or* if your lace fabric has a removable extra side border continue with steps 3 and 4.

3 Remove the border by pulling it off. Turn up 6 mm (¼ in) to the right side at the bottom of the curtain. Tack the hem in place and then press it.

4 Machine stitch the border lace over the turning using zigzag stitch and matching thread. Neaten the edges in line with the sides.

TIP BOX

To use a heading tape and hooks for a track with runners or the direct contact-fixing method, add only 6 cm (2⅜ in) to the length, for the hem. Turn 1 cm (⅜ in) to the wrong side and place the heading tape 3 mm (⅛ in) from the top edge. Stitch in place according to the manufacturer's instructions.

CURTAIN ACCESSORIES

Curtain accessories such as tie-backs, pelmets and valances add a special finishing touch and help to create a fully co-ordinated look. This section gives a choice of tie-backs – ruched, plaited and edged – one of which will suit most room settings. Tie-backs can be made to match the curtains or they can link with other items in the room. A formal pelmet or a gathered valance with contact heading tape for a quick and easy fixing method is also explained here, as well as instructions for making a single swag and pleated tails.

QUICKIE TIE-BACKS

Tie-backs are an ideal way to co-ordinate your curtains with other furnishings in the room. This tie-back is quick and easy to make with a heading tape across a double piece of fabric.

1 For each tie-back, cut out a piece of fabric 25 cm (10 in) wide by twice the required finished length.

2 Turn in each long side of the strip of fabric to the right side, so that the raw edges meet down the centre and pin in place. Machine stitch across each end. Remove the pins, turn right side out and press.

4 Pull up the cords of the tape until the tie-back is the required length. Tie the cords securely and tuck them away at the back.

3 Pin the heading tape in place over the raw edges, turning under 1.2 cm ($\frac{1}{2}$ in) at each end of the tape to neaten. Machine stitch, working in the same direction along both edges. Remove the pins as you stitch.

5 Blanket stitch the curtain rings to the reverse side of the tie-back, about 2 cm ($\frac{3}{4}$ in) from each end.

CHECK LIST

Materials

fabric
standard heading tape – length same as fabric
two rings
general sewing equipment   page 134

Techniques

machine stitching   page 140
blanket stitch   page 139

Measuring up

See page 154.

EDGED TIE-BACK

This style of tie-back goes well with a pelmet and consists of a crescent-shaped piece of fusible buckram covered with fabric. A decorative binding is added all round the edge and the material used for the binding could match the pelmet material or co-ordinate with other furnishings in the room. You can buy a ready-made shape or use the template given on page 154.

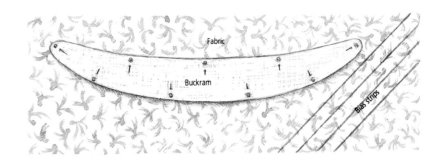

1 Cut out the main fabric using the crescent-shaped piece of buckram as a guide. Cut bias strips 2.5 cm (1 in) wide for the binding. Join the strips to make a sufficient length to go all round the shape.

2 Position the buckram on the wrong side of a piece of lining, and place the cut tie-back right side up over the buckram. Press with a hot iron and damp pressing cloth to fuse them together. Trim off the surplus lining fabric round the buckram shape, taking care not to cut into the buckram.

3 Fold 6 mm ($\frac{1}{4}$ in) to the wrong side at one end of the strip of binding. With right sides facing and raw edges even, pin the turned-in edge of the binding to the curve of the tie-back and continue pinning all round.

4 Machine stitch binding to tie-back 6 mm ($\frac{1}{4}$ in) from the edge all the way round, turning under and overlapping remaining raw edge of binding. Remove pins as you stitch.

5 Fold binding over the raw edge of the tie-back to the reverse side. Turn the raw edge of the binding under by 6 mm ($\frac{1}{4}$ in) and slipstitch to the lining. Blanket stitch the rings to the reverse side of the tie-back, about 2 cm ($\frac{3}{4}$ in) from each end.

PLAITED TIE-BACK

Three padded fabric tubes are plaited together to make this attractive tie-back. It looks best if two of the tubes are made in the same fabric and the third in a contrasting colour. Or, make two strips in a plain fabric and the third in a patterned fabric echoing another material in the room.

1 For each tie-back, cut three fabric strips 10 cm (4 in) wide by 1½ times the required finished length. Cut three lining strips 15 cm (6 in) wide by the same length as the fabric. Cut three pieces of wadding 12 cm (4¾ in) wide and 4 cm (1½ in) shorter than the lining.

2 Place the wadding against the wrong side of the lining, with the edges aligned on one long edge. Roll up the lining and wadding together.

3 Turn under 1 cm (⅜ in) on the remaining long edge of the lining and slipstitch down along the centre of the roll. Stitch across the ends with a small tacking stitch.

4 Secure a length of piping cord to the main fabric strip by machine stitching it to one short end, on the right side.

5 Fold the strip in half lengthways, right sides together, enclosing the cord. Machine stitch the raw edges together along the long side. Turn right side out by pulling the cord, then snip the cord close to the fabric edge.

6 Stitch one end of the cord to the padded roll and the other to a large-eyed, long blunt needle or bodkin.

9 Bind each end with a 10 cm (4 in) square piece of main fabric. Fold the square in half, wrong sides together. Align the raw edges with those at the end of the plait and machine stitch together.

7 Insert the needle/bodkin into the fabric tube at one end and pull the padded roll through it. Snip off the cord. Repeat steps 2–7 to make the other two padded strips.

10 Fold in one end of the binding square, then the other. Turn the folded edge over to cover the machine stitching and slipstitch securely. Remember to make the folds on the same side at each end of the plait.

8 Stitch the three padded strips together overlapping them at one end and then plait them. Stitch them together at the other end to hold the plait securely. Check the tie-back for size.

11 Blanket stitch the rings to the reverse side of the tie-back, about 2 cm (¾ in) from each end.

Plaited tie-backs are a good way to co-ordinate a colour scheme in a room. Use the individual "tubes" to highlight the patterns and colours used on other furnishings in the room.

FRILLED TIE-BACK

This style of tie-back is made with pre-cut iron-on interfacing and could be co-ordinated with a valance or frilled cushions by using a matching or contrasting material for the frill. Iron-on interfacing is used to stiffen the tie-back to give it a professional look. Cut the frill strip in one piece if possible. If it is not possible to do this, cut shorter strips and join them with open seams to get the required length.

C H E C K L I S T

Materials

crescent-shaped iron-on interfacing
fabric
fabric strip for frill
lining
two rings
general sewing equipment   page 134

Techniques

pressing	page 137
open seams	page 142
machine stitching	page 140
slipstitch	page 139
blanket stitch	page 139

Measuring up

See page 154.

1 Using the interfacing shape as a guide, cut out the main fabric for each tie-back, adding 1.5 cm ($\frac{5}{8}$ in) turning allowance all round. For the frill, cut a strip 15 cm (6 in) wide by twice the measurement along the bottom of the interfacing.

2 Cut out the lining using the interfacing as a pattern again and adding on 6 mm ($\frac{1}{4}$ in) turning allowance all round.

3 Position the interfacing with the adhesive side facing the wrong side of the main fabric, making sure that the turning allowance is even all round. Press in position.

4 Join strips of fabric if necessary to make the length of frill required. With right sides facing, fold the frill strip in half lengthways, and machine stitch across each end. Turn right side out and press.

5 Work two rows of machine gathering, 1.5 cm ($\frac{5}{8}$ in) and 6 mm ($\frac{1}{4}$ in) from the raw edge of the frill. Mark the centre and pull up the threads, gathering the frill to fit the bottom of the tie-back 1.5 cm ($\frac{5}{8}$ in) in from each end.

6 Mark the centre of the tie-back. Place the frill over the front of the tie-back, matching the centre marks and with the frill 1.5 cm ($\frac{5}{8}$ in) in from each end. Align the raw edges with the bottom edge of the tie-back and pin in place.

7 Even out the gathers and tack the frill to the tie-back, keeping the stitches close to the edge of the interfacing. Remove pins and machine stitch the frill in place.

Frilled tie-backs are ideal for bedrooms or pretty cottage-style rooms. If in a bedroom, co-ordinate with frilled pillowcases. For a plain curtain fabric, make the tie-back in a patterned material for a splash of colour.

8 Trim the seam. Turn the frill down and tack. Turn and tack the seam allowance along the straight edge and sides.

10 Place the lining wrong side down on the reverse side of the tie-back. Pin and then slipstitch the lining in place.

9 Prepare the lining by turning under to the wrong side 1 cm (⅜ in) all round. Tack in place and then press.

11 Blanket stitch the rings to the reverse side of the tie-back about 2 cm (¾ in) from each end.

RUCHED TIE-BACK

A padded fabric roll is made in the same way as for the plaited tie-back, and this is inserted into a longer tube of fabric, which is then gathered up to create an elegant ruched effect.

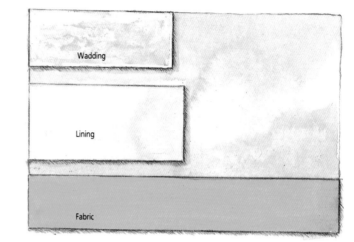

1 For each tie-back, cut out a strip of the main fabric 15 cm (6 in) wide by twice the required finished length. Cut out the lining 20 cm (8 in) wide by the final length required. Cut out the wadding 16 cm (6½ in) wide and 3 cm (1¼ in) shorter than the lining.

2 Place the wadding against the wrong side of the lining, with the edges aligned on one long edge. Roll up the lining and wadding together.

3 Turn under 1 cm (⅜ in) on the remaining long edge of the lining and slipstitch down along the centre of the roll. Stitch across the ends with a small tacking stitch.

4 Secure a length of piping cord to the main fabric strip by machine stitching it to one short end, on the right side.

5 Fold the strip in half lengthways, right sides together, enclosing the cord. Machine stitch the raw edges together along the long side. Turn right side out by pulling the cord, then snip the cord close to the fabric edge.

6 Stitch one end of the cord to the padded roll and the other to a large-eyed, long blunt needle or bodkin.

For that special touch, a ruched tie-back in a single fabric adds texture and visual impact. Use a contrasting fabric or, for a plain curtain, make the tie-back in the same material as the main upholstery.

7 Insert the needle/bodkin into the fabric tube at one end. Pull the padded roll through the tube until the end of the roll is level with the beginning of the fabric tube.

9 Keep pulling the cord, ruching the fabric at the same time, until the padded roll emerges at the other end. Pin in place then cut off the cord close to the edge and neaten the end as in step 8.

8 Neaten the end of the tube by turning in the two corners. Then turn the end over twice and slipstitch neatly. Make sure the roll is securely attached to the end of the fabric tube.

10 Blanket stitch the rings to the reverse side of the tie-back about 2 cm (¾ in) from each end.

SINGLE SWAG

The instructions given here are for a single swag. Make a sample swag and tail using lining fabric or sheeting to help calculate the fabric.

C H E C K   L I S T

Materials

fabric see below
lining see below
touch-and-close fastener
general sewing equipment   page 134

Techniques

cutting	page 136
tacking	page 138
slipstitch	page 138
zigzag stitch	page 141
pressing	page 137
attaching touch-and-close fastener	page 146

Measuring up

Measure the length of the pelmet board and the returns from wall to wall, and the curtain drop. The finished top of the swag should equal the length of the pelmet board and the drop should be approximately one-sixth of the curtain drop. Once you have decided on the finished size of the swag, follow the diagram for the proportions

A to B = ½ finished width
C to D = 2½ times finished drop
E to F = 1½ times finished width. Note this line is three-quarters down from the top of the cut drop measurement.

1 Place the lining right side down on a cutting board or squared paper, and align the selvedge with a straight line along the length of the board.

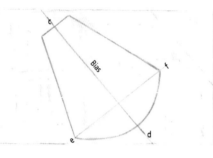

2 Mark out the swag shape on the lining with tailor's chalk or fabric pen, starting with the bias line CD and following the dimensions on the Measuring up diagram. Add a seam allowance of 1.2 cm (½ in) on the curved edge.

3 Cut out the shape and use this to cut the main fabric, ensuring that the centre line is on the bias. Cut a binding strip 10 cm (4 in) deep by the width of the finished swag plus 3 cm (1¼ in).

4 With right sides together, machine stitch the lining and fabric along the curve, 1.2 cm (½ in) from the raw edges. Trim the seam and snip out V's, turn right sides out and press. Tack the sides and top.

5 Pin the binding strip to a suitable surface such as an ironing board, with the long side projecting 2.5 cm (1 in) over the edge. Mark the centre point and a turning allowance of 1.5 cm (⅝ in) at each end with pins.

6 Mark the centre point of the swag and pin the swag to the strip, matching the centres. Pleat the long sides evenly up to the binding strip starting at point F and working on one side at a time.

7 About four pleats on each side will take up the fullness of the material. The pleats on either side of the centre go across the straight top edge of the swag and points E and F will touch the end pins.

8 Unpin the swag from the binding strip, but replace the pins to hold the pleats as you work across. Tack the pleats in place.

9 With right sides together, place the binding strip along the top of the swag and pin in place. Tack and remove the pins. Machine stitch 1.2 cm ($\frac{1}{2}$ in) from the raw edges.

10 Fold the seam and binding strip to the wrong side. Turn in 1.5 cm ($\frac{5}{8}$ in) at the sides and 1.2 cm ($\frac{1}{2}$ in) along the length. Fold the binding down and slipstitch to cover the stitching.

11 Zigzag stitch the loop side of the touch-and-close fastener tape to the wrong side of the binding. Machine a 15 cm (6 in) length of the hook side of touch-and-close fastener to the right side at each side of the swag to hold the tails.

QUICK SWAG

For a quick and easy yet no less stunning effect, make a simple unlined swag. Measure the length of the pole and the drop at either side and make extra allowance for the depth of the drape required. The simplest way to calculate the amount of fabric needed is to take a length of string and loop it over the pole to imitate the swag.

1 Cut out the fabric and trim away the selvedges. Drape the length of fabric over the pole to assess the effect when the full width is used. Reduce the depth if necessary by cutting the excess from one long edge of the fabric.

2 Make a double hem all round the outside edges by turning 6 mm ($\frac{1}{4}$ in) to the wrong side twice, then pin it in place. Tack the hem, remove the pins and machine stitch close to the tacking and press.

TAILS

Instructions are given for a left-hand tail. To make the right-hand one, reverse the pattern when you cut out the fabric. The tails overlap the swag at each end by 15 cm (6 in).

Measuring up

Note the measurements required following the diagram.
A to B = the drop of the finished swag.
C to D = A to B times 2
C to E and D to F = width of a return (generally 10 cm/4 in).
The instructions are for three pleats using 20 cm (8 in) of fabric per pleat. The fold of the first pleat is placed to the inside edge of the return and the second and third 2.5 cm (1 in) away from the previous pleat.

1 Lay the lining fabric right side down and mark out the dimensions of the tail piece with tailor's chalk or fabric pen, adding a seam allowance of 1.2 cm (½ in) all round.

2 Cut out the shape and use this to cut the main fabric. Cut a binding strip 10 cm (4 in) deep by the width of the finished tail.

4 Turn right sides out and press the edges. Tack the fabric and lining together across the raw top edge.

3 Place the main fabric and lining right sides together, and machine stitch round the sides and bottom edge 1.2 cm (½ in) from the raw edges. Trim the seams and corners.

5 Mark the position of the pleats and the spaces between them with pins along the top and bottom edges of the tail following the measurements given.

6 Form three pleats, starting at the short edge, pressing them in place as you go. Press a fold down the line (E to F) where the tail will turn around the corner of the pelmet board.

7 Place the binding strip right side down across the right side of the top of the tail and pin in place. Tack, removing the pins as you work. Machine stitch 1.2 cm (½ in) from the raw edges.

8 Press the seam and strip upwards on the wrong side. Turn in 1.5 cm (⅝ in) at the sides and 1.2 cm (½ in) along the length. Fold the binding down and slipstitch in place, covering the machine stitching.

9 Machine the loop side of touch-and-close fastener tape to the wrong side of the binding across the front face of the tail using zigzag stitch.

10 Make a diagonal fold in the binding to form a corner for the side return and attach a strip of fastener with zigzag stitch to the wrong side of the side return.

11 Make a right-hand side tail in the same way, but reversing the sides on the diagram.

FIXING A SWAG AND TAILS IN PLACE

Press the hook side of the touch-and-close fastener to the top of the pelmet board and returns. Place the swag in position and press the fastener tape on the swag firmly against the tape on the pelmet board. Then attach the tails over the swag to the top of the pelmet board at each side and round the returns. A thumb tack at each side will keep them securely in position.

PELMETS

The instructions given here on how to make a pelmet uses a double-sided self-adhesive stiffener, which is an easy method that produces good results. A variety of shapes are printed on the peel-off backing paper.

C H E C K   L I S T

Materials

self-adhesive pelmet stiffener
fabric
lining
self-adhesive hook tape
general sewing equipment   page 134
braid (optional) and fabric glue

Techniques

cutting	page 136
machine stitching	page 140
mitred corners	page 144
zigzag stitch	page 141
slipstitch	page 139

Measuring up

To estimate how big your pelmet is, measure the length of the pelmet board from A to B and the returns, B to C, plus the depth, D to E.

1 Cut out the fabric using the stiffener as a template, adding on 2 cm ($\frac{3}{4}$ in) all round. Mark the centre points of both fabric and stiffener.

2 Cut out the lining to the exact size of the pelmet stiffener shape at the bottom and sides, but add on an extra 2.5 cm (1 in) at the top.

3 Start peeling the backing paper off the stiffener, working from the centre. Place the fabric wrong side down on the adhesive, matching centres. Continue to peel away the backing, smoothing down the fabric with your hand as you go to prevent puckering.

4 Turn the pelmet over and snip the curves of the turning allowance, but not right up to the edge of the stiffener. Cut the corners away. Peel off the backing paper from the reverse side of the stiffener.

5 Press down the turning allowance with your fingers, making neat mitres at the corners.

6 Turn 2.5 cm (1 in) at the top and 9 mm ($\frac{3}{8}$ in) along the bottom and the sides to the wrong side of the lining and press in place.

7 Position a strip of the loop side of the self-adhesive fastener along the right-side top edge of the lining. Machine stitch with zigzag stitch along both edges of the fastener.

10 Press the hook side of the self-adhesive fastener to the front edge of the pelmet board. Starting in the centre, attach the pelmet by firmly pressing together the self-adhesive fastener.

8 Mark the centre of the lining on the right side, and the pelmet on the wrong side.

11 If wanted, apply a co-ordinating trimming braid using a fabric glue once the pelmet is in position.

9 Place the lining carefully over the back of the pelmet, wrong side down, aligning the centre marks. Smooth the lining on the adhesive as before. Slipstitch the lining to the fabric around the edges.

Pelmets give an added dimension to windows whatever the size and style of the room. Choose a shape that suits the room, from a simple square shape to the more elaborate styles used for larger windows and the more exotic, heavier curtains. Above is a selection of possible pelmet shapes. You may want the shape of the pelmet to echo a shape in the curtain fabric. However, whatever size or style you choose, always ensure there is enough space between the pelmet and the curtain track to allow the curtains to be used freely.

Once you have chosen your pelmet, cover it in a fabric that either matches the curtains or that contrasts with the curtains and co-ordinates with other fabrics in the room.

VALANCES

Valances are like mini curtains. To determine the desired length, cut a length of paper or spare fabric about one-sixth of the curtain drop and tape it to the curtain to check the effect.

C H E C K L I S T

Materials

fabric	page 54
lining	
pencil pleat heading tape with loop backing	
self-adhesive hook tape	
general sewing equipment	page 134

Techniques

cutting	page 136
open seams	page 142
mitred corners	page 144
machine stitching	page 140
pressing	page 137
slipstitch	page 139
tacking	page 138
attaching heading tape	page 52

Measuring up

Measure the length of the valance shelf or rail and the returns from wall to wall. Calculate the width of fabric needed to give the correct fullness in the same way as for curtains. Decide on the depth of the valance in proportion to the length of the curtains and add 4 cm (1½ in).

1 Cut out the required number of widths from the curtain fabric adding 4 cm (1½ in) to the finished depth. Cut out lining to the size of the finished valance omitting turning allowance. Join widths of fabric and lining if necessary.

2 Lay the fabric right side down and turn in 2.5 cm (1 in) along the bottom and side edges. Pin in place. Press and remove the pins. Form a mitre in each bottom corner.

3 Machine stitch the mitres from the fold to 1 cm (⅜ in) from the raw edges. Trim the corner away. Turn the valance right side out and press the corners again.

4 With the lining right side up, place the valance over it, right side down. Align the bottom raw edges, and pin them together. Machine stitch 1 cm (⅜ in) from the edges and remove pins.

5 Turn the lining over to the wrong side of the valance and press the fold. Trim off 6 mm (¼ in) from the sides and top edge of the lining.

6 Turn the lining under by 1 cm (⅜ in) at the sides. Pin the side hems, slipstitch, then press.

As valances are not moved they can be hung in many different ways. Make a cased heading for a "dress" curtain. Or hang a valance on a plain wooden rod with matching rings for a more informal look at windows or on a simple four-poster bed.

7 Tack down the lining, which should be 1.5 cm (⅝ in) shorter than the valance, along the top. Turn the 1.5 cm (⅝ in) heading allowance over the lining and press the fold.

9 Machine stitch along the tape working in the same direction along both edges and stitch the turned in ends. Gather the valance to the required length by pulling up the cords. Knot the ends and tuck them away at the back.

8 Position the heading tape just below the top of the valance, and turn 1.5 cm (⅝ in) under at each end of the tape. Make sure the cords are free. Pin the tape in place.

10 Fix the self-adhesive hook-side of the tape to the front edge of the valance shelf and press the loop backing of the heading tape to it, starting from the centre and working outwards.

BLINDS

Blinds are a practical and economical way of covering windows and this section gives instructions for Roman, balloon and Austrian blinds. The Roman blind has a flat tailored appearance making it an ideal choice above a kitchen sink or a worktop, and when raised allows maximum daylight to enter the room. The balloon blind has inverted pleats which when raised balloon out quite magically. The extra fullness from the gathered heading of an Austrian blind gives a more luxurious appearance.

we need your help to reduce
the drastic impact of the

**ASH DIEBACK
DISEASE**

incurable disease is
ected to wipe out up to

50%

Here in Gloucestershire
we are likely to see the
loss of *hundreds of
thousands* of ash
trees

MEASURING FOR BLINDS

BLINDS ARE often a more practical alternative to window dressing than curtains – they use less fabric and are relatively simple to make.

Absolute accuracy at all stages is essential when measuring up, but especially when cutting the fabric, if the blind is to hang true. Lining is advisable, as it makes the finished blind hang better, protects the fabric and improves insulation.

Note the instructions for measuring up different types of blinds to work out positions for the seams that make them as unobtrusive as possible.

When working with fabric joins, make sure that the seams of the lining will correspond exactly with those of the main fabric, to avoid an unsightly appearance when light shows through from the back.

For the Roman blind, if you do need to make joins in the fabric to obtain the correct width required, ensure you have a full width in the centre, with the extra fabric joined at either side.

The three blinds shown in this section hang in slightly different ways, though the making up methods are similar. It is important to choose a fabric appropriate to the style of blind – firmly woven curtain fabric is ideal for Roman or balloon blinds, while light/medium weight material is better suited to ruche and form the swags that distinguish an Austrian blind.

Positioning the batten

All the blinds in this section are attached at the top of the window to a wooden batten. Each blind is drawn up by a series of vertical cords threaded through rings sewn on the reverse side. When the blind is raised, the cords are secured by winding them in a figure of eight around a cleat which is screwed to the side wall. To conceal the batten, paint it or cover in fabric.

For the batten, you will need a 50 mm × 25 mm (2 in × 1 in) piece of softwood, cut to the required length and fixed to the head of the window with angle brackets.

For fitting within a recess, the blind should be made 2.5 cm (1 in) narrower, so that it will fit neatly inside it. The batten should then be fixed to the ceiling of the recess, (not suitable for a Balloon blind) and the drop of the blind measured from the ceiling to the sill.

If the batten is to be fixed on the wall above the window cut the batten long enough to extend 5 cm (2 in) on either side.

Measuring up

To calculate the finished width of the blind, measure the length of the batten.

• To calculate the finished length of the blind, measure from the top of the batten to the sill. For a blind fixed within a recess, deduct 2 cm ($\frac{3}{4}$ in) to allow for clearance above the sill. If it is to be positioned outside the window add 10 cm (4 in), so the blind will fall that distance from the bottom of the sill.

• Check your measurements at several points on the window frame to ensure it is square.

ROMAN BLINDS

TO FORM THE DISTINCTIVE pleats of a Roman blind, horizontal channels are stitched at regular intervals down its length, through which narrow rods or laths are inserted. These give a more professional-looking, tailored appearance when the blind is drawn up.

• Calculate the finished length and width of the blind and add 2.5 cm (1 in) turning allowances all round.

• For the lining, the width will be exactly the same as the finished width of the blind, but extra length is required to allow for the channels which are stitched across the lining to hold the laths or rods. This extra length is based on how many channels you want.

• To calculate the exact number of channels required for the size of your blind, make a plan (see left), dividing the length into sections as follows: mark the first line 15 cm (6 in) up from the bottom, mark the centre lines 30 cm (12 in) apart, and allow an extra 8 cm (3 in) above the position of the final one for the top section. You may need to adjust the sizes of the spaces slightly to accommodate the finished length of the blind.

• Once you have decided on the number of channels, add an extra 6 cm (2¼ in) to the length for each one. (Note: the size of the channel quoted here allows for the use of 2.5 cm × 4 mm (1 in × ⅛ in) wooden laths. If you are using wooden or plastic rods with a diameter of less than 2.5 cm (1 in), reduce the size of the channels accordingly.) Finally, add a further 2.5 cm (1 in) top turning allowance to give you the total length for the lining fabric.

FIXING A ROMAN BLIND

Fix screw eyes to the batten so that they correspond exactly with the rows of rings on the blind. Fix an extra one 2.5 cm (1 in) from the edge of the batten on the operating side.

• Attach the hook side of the fastener to the front of the batten and press the tapes together to fix the blind in position. Thread the cords through the screw eyes and knot them together just outside the last one. Cut the ends level, and attach an acorn to hold the cord ends together. Screw the cleat in position on the wall.

8 cm (3 in)

30 cm (12 in)

30 cm (12 in)

30 cm (12 in)

30 cm (12 in)

15 cm (6 in)

BALLOON BLINDS

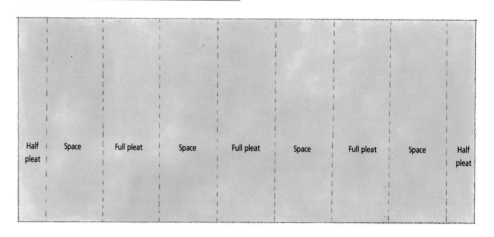

TO CREATE THE FULLNESS needed for the inverted pleats of a balloon blind, it will be necessary to join widths of fabric. By carefully planning the positioning of the pleats the seam lines can be concealed by a fold. The allowance for the length takes into account the extra fabric required for the bottom swags which are ruched permanently.

• Follow the guidance for positioning the batten and note the finished width and length required for the blind.

• Make a plan (see right) for the position of the pleats, allowing 30 cm (12 in) for a full pleat and 15 cm (6 in) for the half pleats at either side of the blind. Allow a 30 cm (12 in) space between the centres of each pleat and divide the finished width of the blind by this

measurement to give you the number of pleats that will be required. You may need to adjust the measurements slightly to accommodate the finished width in relation to the width of fabric used – make your alteration to the size allowed for the spaces rather than the pleats.

• Once you have calculated the width of fabric required, add on 8 cm (3¼ in) for side turnings and 3 cm (1¼ in) for each joining seam. Add 30 cm (12 in) to the finished drop measurement.

• The measurement for the lining fabric is the same as the curtain fabric.

Roman blind

Balloon blind

AUSTRIAN BLINDS

AUSTRIAN BLINDS have a more lavish appearance, due to their extra fullness – at least twice the width of the batten is needed. If it is necessary to join widths, the seams will be less obtrusive if they are joined where a row of rings will be sewn. Note that, like balloon blinds, the length allowance takes into account the extra fabric for the bottom swags.

• Follow the guidance for positioning the batten and note the finished width and length required.

• You will need at least twice the width in fabric and an extra 30 cm (12 in) (see right) added to the length. Allow a 60 cm (24 in) space between the rings in the ungathered material, and add a further 5 cm (2 in) either side. Bear in mind the approximate position of the rings before working out the quantity of fabric and where the seaming will

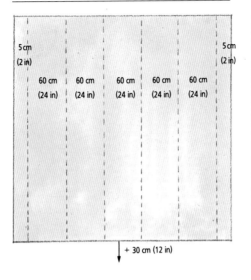

be. If frills are to be added, remember to make allowance by reducing the length measurement of the blind by the depth of the frill, but allow for sufficient fabric to make the frill.

• The measurement for the lining is the same as the main fabric.

FIXING

Fix screw eyes to the batten so that they correspond exactly with the rows of rings on the blind. Fix an extra screw 2.5 cm (1 in) from the edge on the operating side (left or right) of the blind. For a balloon blind attach the hook side of the fastener to the top of the batten and press the tapes together to fix the blind in position so that it hangs over the edge. For an Austrian blind, attach the hook side of the fastener to the front of the batten and pull up the heading tape cords to gather to fit the batten.

Thread the cords through the screw eyes, and knot them together just outside the last one. Cut the ends level, plait the loose cords if desired, and attach an acorn to hold the cord ends together. Screw the cleat in position on the wall. To keep the bottom permanently ruched raise the blind to the desired drop measurement and wind the cords around the cleat. Tie or sew two or more of the rings together on the vertical rows.

Austrian blind

ROMAN BLINDS

A firmly woven fabric is the best choice for a Roman blind, and it should be lined. Roman blinds are easy to make, but it is very important to transfer the measurements accurately at all stages to make sure that the blind hangs straight. Also, always position one of the rows of rings down the centre, even if the blind is narrow.

CHECK LIST

Materials

fabric
lining
wooden rods
rings as required
cord
25 mm (1 in) wide touch-and-close fastener
screw eyes
cleat
general sewing equipment   page 134

Techniques

Measuring up

For the amount of fabric, lining, dowelling and cord required, see page 90.

1 Make sure that the cut edges of the fabric and lining are straight and at right angles to the selvedges. Trim off the selvedges. Cut and join the fabric lengths and lining lengths if necessary with open seams.

2 Turn 2.5 cm (1 in) to the wrong side on the sides and bottom of the main fabric and pin in place. Press the hems and form a mitre in each bottom corner, removing pins.

3 Re-pin the side and bottom hems on the right side and topstitch 1.5 cm ($\frac{5}{8}$ in) from the folded edges, removing pins as you stitch.

4 Turn 1.2 cm ($\frac{1}{2}$ in) to the wrong side on the sides and bottom of the lining and pin in place. Press the hems and machine stitch removing, the pins as you stitch.

5 Lay the lining down right side up on a flat surface and mark the stitching lines for the rod channels based on your measurements.

6 Bring the marked lines together to form the channels on the right side and pin and tack them. Remove the pins and take out tacking. Machine stitch each channel and take out tacking.

7 Lay the main fabric right side down and the lining over it right side up. Align the raw edges at the top. The lining will be 1.2 cm (½ in) smaller than the main fabric at the sides and bottom.

8 Carefully smooth out the lining, making sure that it stays square to the main fabric. Pin the two fabrics together along the bottom edge of the lining and then alongside the stitching for the rod channels, working up from the bottom.

9 Tack along the bottom and along the stitching lines for the rod channels. Machine stitch along the rod channels only, making sure that the lines are horizontal and parallel to each other.

10 Pin the sides of the lining to the blind between the channels. Slipstitch the lining to the blind along the sides and bottom edge.

11 Tack the raw edges of the fabric and lining together across the top. Turn down 2.5 cm (1 in) to the wrong side and pin. Machine the "loop" side of fastener over the raw edges with zigzag stitch, removing pins as you stitch.

12 Insert a rod into each channel and stitch across the ends of each channel to hold the rods in place.

13 Position the cording rings on the folded edges of the channels 7.5 cm (3 in) in from each side and at intervals of approximately 30 cm (12 in) across the width of the blind. Stitch the rings in place.

14 Cut the required number of lengths of cord, allowing sufficient for threading through the screw eyes and down the operating side when fixing the blind in place. Knot a length of cord firmly to each bottom ring, and then thread the cords through the vertical rows of rings. Fix the blind in place.

BALLOON BLINDS

A balloon blind is a combination of a Roman blind and an Austrian blind. It is flat at the top and ruched into swags at the bottom, and is made with extra width in the fabric, which allows inverted pleats to be formed and pressed.

1 Cut the fabric and lining into drop lengths, based on your measurements. Trim off the selvedges and join lengths with open seams, matching patterns if necessary.

2 Lay the main fabric right side up and mark the spaces, pleats and side allowances with pins, making sure that any seams will be under a pleat fold.

3 Cut off the surplus width on both the main fabric and lining, taking a further 5 cm (2 in) from each side of the lining. Remove the marker pins from the top of the main fabric. Mark the centre of both the fabric and lining, top and bottom, with a pin.

4 With right sides together, align the raw edges of the main fabric and lining at the sides and pin. Machine stitch 1.5 cm ($\frac{5}{8}$ in) from the edges, removing pins as you stitch. Press the seam open.

5 With the lining uppermost match the centre pins, leaving an equal margin of main fabric visible at each side. Pin the bottom edges together, and machine stitch 1.2 cm (½ in) from the raw edges. Trim the corners. Remove the pins.

6 Turn right side out and press the sides, so that an equal amount of the main fabric shows at each side. Smooth out the blind right side up on a flat surface and tack the top raw edges together.

7 Check the pleat and space measurements on your plan and re-mark with pins along the top and opposite along the bottom. Form the pleats, pin them in place, then press along the fold lines.

8 Machine down the inside of each pleat for 10 cm (4 in) from the top. Re-press the pleats and then stitch straight across each one to secure them in place.

9 Turn under 1.5 cm (⅝ in) to the wrong side along the top of the blind and pin. Machine the "loop" side of the fastener tape with zigzag stitch over the raw edge removing pins as you stitch.

10 Position the cording rings along the centre of each pleat, starting 5 cm (2 in) from the bottom and finishing 25 cm (10 in) from the fastener tape. Space the remainder approximately 15 cm (6 in) apart. Stitch the rings firmly in place through both the fabric and lining.

11 Knot a length of cord firmly to each bottom ring, and then thread the cords through the vertical rows of rings. Fix the blind in place. To keep swags permanently ruched at desired height, raise the blind and tie or sew two or more of the rings together on each of the vertical rows at the back of the blind.

AUSTRIAN BLINDS

An Austrian blind is gathered across the top using a pencil-pleat heading tape, and when drawn up it ruches upwards forming deep swags across the width of the blind. A frill added to the bottom and sides of the blind can give a luxurious and feminine look to a bedroom, while a frill across the bottom can be used to contrast with other furnishings in the room.

C H E C K   L I S T

Materials

fabric
lining
touch-and-close fastener
rings as required
cord
pencil-pleat heading tape
screw eyes
cleat
general sewing equipment   page 134

Techniques

open seams	page 142
frills	page 150
machine stitching	page 140
tacking	page 138
fixing in place	page 93
pressing	page 137

Measuring up

For fabric, lining, fastener, ring, cord and heading tape requirements, see page 93.

1 Cut the fabric and lining into drop lengths. Trim off the selvedges and measure precisely the widths you require from your calculated measurements, and cut off the surplus.

2 Join the fabric widths together with open seams, and do the same for the lining widths. Trim 5 cm (2 in) from both the side edges of the lining. Mark the centre of each with a pin.

3 Make up the frill and apply to the bottom of the main fabric, placing the neatened ends of the frill 4 cm (1⅝ in) from the side edges. Machine stitch in place 1.5 cm (⅝ in) from the raw edges.

4 Tack the frill up on the right side of the blind to keep it out of the way.

5 Place the fabric and lining right sides together (remember that the fabric is larger than the lining), align the side edges, pin and tack together. Remove the pins, machine stitch and press the seam open.

6 Matching the centre marks, smooth out the lining and position it over the frill seam, leaving an equal margin of the main fabric visible at each side. Pin across the bottom of the blind, tack, and remove the pins.

7 Turn the blind over and machine across the bottom, following the row of stitching from attaching the frill. Trim the seam and the corners.

8 Turn the blind right sides out and release frill tacking thread. Tack the fabric and lining together across the top. Press the blind. Remove centre pins.

9 Turn under 1.5 cm ($\frac{5}{8}$ in) to the wrong side at the top of the blind and attach the pencil-pleat contact heading tape with a straight machine stitch over the raw edges.

10 Position the cording rings starting 5 cm (2 in) from the frill seam and finishing 30 cm (12 in) from the heading tape. Space the remainder approximately 20 cm (8 in) apart. The outside rows should start 5 cm (2 in) from the side edges.

11 Stitch the rings firmly in place through both the fabric and lining. Knot a length of cord firmly to each bottom ring, and then thread the cords through the vertical rows of rings. Fix the blind in place.

FESTOON BLINDS

Festoon blinds are constructed in the same way as Austrian blinds. The difference is that twice the length of fabric is required, and instead of sewing on rings, you machine stitch a special festoon-blind tape in place of the rows of rings. Pull up the ruching cords incorporated in the tape and knot them to give the desired drop length. Then insert rings into the tape, according to the manufacturer's instructions, thread cords through these to raise and lower the blinds (if required).

Lightweight fabrics give a better result for these blinds. They can be made of a sheer fabric, and can be used as an alternative to nets.

CUSHIONS

Cushions can be made in a variety of shapes and sizes, and provide added comfort as well as being a decorative feature which can link the colours in a room. As only a small amount of fabric is required, it is possible to experiment with different types of fabrics and colours and to use off-cuts from other projects. Instructions are given for making heart-shaped, round, square, bolster and box cushions, with suggestions for different methods of fastenings and trimmings.

SELF-BORDERED CUSHION

This style of cushion would look good in a living room or bedroom. It is easy to make as the border is included with the cover when cutting out, and touch-and-close fastener is used. Instructions are given for a standard cushion-pad size, for non-standard, see Measuring up below.

C H E C K L I S T

Materials

40 cm (16 in) cushion pad
60 cm (24 in) of 122 cm (48 in) wide fabric
30 cm (12 in) touch-and-close fastener
general sewing equipment   page 134

Techniques

cutting	page 136
tacking	page 138
zigzag stitch	page 141
machine stitching	page 140
pressing	page 137
attaching touch-and-close	page 146

Measuring up

To calculate the amount of fabric required for a non-standard cushion, measure the cushion pad as shown adding 10 cm (4 in) to each measurement for the front and an extra 7.5 cm (3 in) to one measurement for the back opening.

1 Lay the fabric right side down and mark the cutting lines for one front piece and two back pieces with tailor's chalk. Cut out the pieces.

2 Turn 2.5 cm (1 in) to the wrong side along the centre edges of one back piece and pin. Tack the hem, remove the pins and neaten the raw edge with zigzag stitch. Repeat with second back piece. Press the hems.

4 Stitch the loop side to the wrong side of the other back piece, making sure the two sides will be aligned when fastened.

3 Stitch the hook side of the touch-and-close fastener to the right side of one back piece, positioning it an equal distance from each end.

5 With the touch-and-close strips fastened, machine stitch across the ends of the opening.

6 Place the front and back of the cover right sides together and pin round all four sides. Tack round the four sides and remove the pins. Machine stitch all round 1.3 cm ($\frac{1}{2}$ in) from the raw edges.

7 Trim the seam close to the stitching, and clip across the corners. Turn the cover right side out and press.

8 With the back of the cushion-cover fastened, mark a stitching line with tailor's chalk round all four sides 5 cm (2 in) from the outer edges. Top stitch along the line and remove pins. Press the cover and insert the pad.

Self-bordered cushions are attractive and easy to sew. Make them all in the same fabric to co-ordinate with other furnishings in the room or, if you have plain upholstery, make each cushion in a different colour for maximum impact.

ROUND PIPED CUSHION

The cushion cover shown here is trimmed with piping. You could attach a frill to co-ordinate with the curtains or upholstery. Instructions are for a standard cushion-pad size, for non-standard, see Measuring up.

CHECK LIST

Materials

paper for pattern
40 cm (16 in) cushion pad
60 cm (24 in) of 122 cm (48 in) wide fabric
1.30 m (52 in) No. 3 piping cord (pre-shrink)
30 cm (12 in) zip
general sewing equipment   page 134

Techniques

making a pattern	page 154
cutting	page 136
tacking	page 138
machine stitching	page 140
inserting a zip	page 147
piping	page 149
pressing	page 137

Measuring up

Measure the diameter of the cushion pad, and make a pattern from a square piece of paper 1 cm ($\frac{1}{2}$ in) larger than this measurement.

1 Pin the circle patterns to the fabric, marking the zip seam allowance directly on the material.

2 Cut out the fabric for the cushion cover, cutting along the zip seam on the back piece. Cut bias strips for the piping.

3 To join the back pieces, place them right sides together. Pin them along the zip seam, then tack them together 1.5 cm ($\frac{5}{8}$ in) from the raw edges. Remove pins.

4 Machine stitch along the zip seam for 5 cm (2 in) in from each side. Machine tack the centre section and press seams open. Insert the zip.

5 Join the bias strips for piping to make a length equal to the circumference of the cushion plus 2.5 cm (1 in). Make the piping and attach to the front cover piece. Join the ends of the piping.

8 Trim the seam and snip out 'V's all round being careful not to cut into the stitching.

9 Turn the cover right sides out, press and insert the cushion pad. Close zip.

6 With the zip partly open, place the front and back pieces right sides together, and pin them all round the edge. Tack all round and remove the pins.

7 With the front piece uppermost, machine stitch all round, following the line of stitching from applying the piping.

Piping can be used on a cushion to contrast with the main colour or to tone with a patterned fabric. Piping also helps to define the shape of a cushion, especially if there are several cushions stacked together.

HEART-SHAPED CUSHION

This an ideal cushion for a romantic bedroom style. For an extra-special look, use contrasting ribbon to trim the finished cover, either hand stitching tiny bows or roses to the front, or threading a narrow length of ribbon through an eyelet-type broderie anglaise frill. Because of its shape, it is necessary to make the cushion pad yourself.

CHECKLIST

Materials

squared paper – see template	page 156
cushion pad: 50 cm (20 in) of 90 cm (36 in) wide thin cotton fabric	
medium-sized bag of polyester filling	
cushion cover: 50 cm (20 in) of 90 cm (36 in) wide fabric	
2 m (6 ft 9 in) of 6 cm (2⅜ in) wide broderie anglaise trim	
3 poppa-snaps	
general sewing equipment	page 134

Techniques

cutting	page 136
tacking	page 138
machine stitching	page 140
slipstitch	page 139
seams	page 142
zigzag stitch	page 141
top stitch	page 141
attaching poppa-snaps	page 147
pressing	page 137

1 To make the cushion pad, cut out two pieces from the thin cotton fabric using the pattern on page 156. Add 1 cm (⅜ in) all round. With right sides facing, pin, then tack the two pieces together and remove pins.

2 Machine stitch 1.3 cm (½ in) from the raw edges, leaving a 4 cm (10 in) opening on one side.

3 Trim the seam. Snip out 'V's, without cutting too close to the stitching, and snip where the shape dips inwards. Turn the cover right side out. Stuff it with filling and slipstitch the gap to close.

4 To make the cover, cut out one piece of fabric to the exact size of the pattern for the front.

5 For the back, cut the pattern into two pieces and place them on the fabric with a gap of 7.5 cm (3 in) between them for the fastening. Cut out the two pieces.

6 To make the frill, join the ends of the broderie anglaise trim with a narrow seam. Zigzag stitch both the edges together to neaten and press to one side.

7 Find the point halfway round the trim from the seam and mark it with a tailor's tack. Gather the frill along the raw edge, breaking off the threads at seam and tailor's tack.

8 Position the frill on the front piece of the cover, with right sides together and raw edges even. Place the frill seam at the top and the tack mark at the bottom of the heart.

9 Pin the frill in place, even out the gathers, tack and machine 1.3 cm (½ in) from raw edges. Tack down the outer edges of the frill to right side of front.

10 To prepare the back, turn under 2.5 cm (1 in) to the wrong side on the cut edges of the opening and zigzag stitch to neaten.

11 Overlap the neatened edges by 2.5 cm (1 in) and top stitch 5 cm (2 in) in from each side. Position and fix poppa-snaps and fasten them. The back should be the same size as the front.

12 Place the back over the front, with right sides together, and raw edges even. Pin, then tack together and remove the pins. Machine stitch with the front uppermost to follow the frill stitching line.

13 Trim the seam, snip 'V's out round the curves and snip towards dip. Turn the cover right side out and remove the tacking to release the trim. Press the cover and insert the cushion pad.

Heart-shaped cushions can be made in a pretty flowered fabric and trimmed with lace for a romantic bedroom look. Add a personal touch with ribbon roses and bows.

SQUARE BOX CUSHION

Box cushions are ideal for co-ordinating garden furniture and window seats.

1 Using your measurements, mark the cutting lines for the top, bottom and welt pieces of the cushion, following the cutting plan. Cut out the pieces and bias strips for the piping.

2 Cut the back welt piece in half lengthways. Insert the zip.

3 With right sides together pin side welt pieces to each end of the back piece. Then pin the other ends of the side welt pieces to each end of the front welt piece.

4 Before stitching, insert cushion pad into joined up welt to check for a snug fit. Tack along pinned seams 1.5 cm (⅝ in) from the raw edges, remove the pins and machine stitch. Press the seams open.

5 Make up sufficient piping to go round the top and bottom pieces of the cushion cover, and apply them to each piece, snipping each corner of the piping skirt.

6 With right sides together and corners matching, pin the welt to the top piece on all four sides.

9 Turn the cover right side out, insert the cushion pad and close the zip.

Cover box cushions in lively bold fabrics which contrast with throw cushions. For a window seat, cover in the same fabric as the curtains. As this cushion is for the seat of a chair, it needs to fit snugly.

7 Tack along the line of piping stitching, remove the pins and machine close to the tacking.

8 With the zip partly open, attach the bottom piece to the welt in the same way. Trim the seams, snip into seam allowances of the welt and cut across the corners.

BOLSTER CUSHION

Bolsters are firm cushions for use on beds and sofas, where a pair is placed at each end. They are cylindrical in shape, made from a block of foam or a very firmly stuffed fabric roll with round ends. Tube-like covers are very easy and quick to make, and the ends can be trimmed with tassels, ribbon or buttons

CHECKLIST

Materials

bolster pad
lightweight fabric – see Measuring up
general sewing equipment   page 134

Techniques

cutting	page 136
machine stitching	page 140
pressing	page 137
making ties	page 146

Measuring up

Measure the length of the bolster and the diameter of one end and add 6 cm (2¼ in). Measure the circumference and add 3 cm (1¼ in).

1 Cut out the fabric required for the bolster cover. From the remaining fabric cut two strips 4 cm (1⅝ in) wide by 1 m 20 cm (47 in).

2 With right sides facing and raw edges even, pin the long edges together. Machine stitch 1.5 cm (⅝ in) from the raw edges. Press the seam open and turn right side out.

3 Turn 1 cm (⅜ in) to the wrong side at one end, pin and press. Turn a further 2 cm (¾ in) to make a double hem, pin and machine stitch. Remove the pins. Press and repeat at other end of fabric tube. Make the fabric ties.

4 Unpick a few of the seam stitches on the right side of the bolster, at the hem end. Attach a safety pin to one end of fabric tie, insert into the opening and thread the strips through the hem casing. Repeat at the other end.

5 Insert the bolster into the cover. It should be a snug fit with an even amount of fabric at each end. Pull up the fabric ties to gather the ends. Tie into bows.

MAKING TASSELS

Tassels can be used to co-ordinate colours and fabrics. Any material is suitable and colours and textures can be mixed for added contrast. Bold tassels can be made from bundles of wool, rolled up pleated fabrics or strips of leather.

1 Cut two pieces of card the length of the tassel. Wind the yarn around the two pieces of card placed together. With two bits of yarn tie one loop through the top of the yarn and thread another piece through this loop several times.

2 At the opposite end cut the yarn between the cards.

3 Bind tassel about 15 mm (½ in) from the top, secure the yarn and leave enough yarn for attaching the tassel.

Tassels, coloured buttons, rosettes, and separate fabric ends can all be added to bolster cushions to help create a co-ordinated look. Buy or make huge rosettes in the same or toning fabric, add a self-covered or contrasting button, or make separate ends in a complementary colour that co-ordinates with other colours in the room.

BED LINEN

Items of bed linen are very easy to make as most of the sewing is just machining straight lines. Instructions in this section give the most simple way to achieve a good professional finish. An easy-care mix-and-match polyester/cotton sheeting can be used for most of the items, including a choice of two methods for making pillowcases, a bed base valance, and a duvet cover made from just stitching two pieces together. The throw-over bedspread is the easiest way of giving a fully co-ordinated look to a bedroom.

PLAIN PILLOWCASE

A standard pillowcase is made from one piece of fabric which can match or contrast with existing bed linen. Larger cushions, say for a teenager's bedroom, can be made in the same way using any practical, easy-to-wash material.

CHECK LIST

Materials

polyester/cotton sheeting – see Measuring up
general sewing equipment   page 134

Techniques

cutting	page 136
tacking	page 138
machine stitching	page 140
French seam	page 143
pressing	page 137

Measuring up

As sizes vary, it is important to measure the pillow in order to calculate the amount of fabric required. Following the diagram, measure the length from A to B, double it, and add 23 cm (9 in) for flap and hem allowance. Measure the width from C to D and add 3 cm (1¼ in) for seams.

1 Cut a piece of fabric on the straight grain to the required length and width.

2 Make a double hem across one short end of the piece of fabric by turning over 6 mm (¼ in) to the wrong side twice, and pin in place. Tack the hem, remove the pins and machine stitch close to the tacking.

4 Turn the raw edge under 6 mm (¼ in) and pin in place. Tack the hem, remove the pins and machine stitch close to the tacking.

5 Lay the piece of fabric right side down. Fold over the end with the narrow hem 16 cm (6¼ in) and pin in place. Press the fold and remove the pins.

3 At the opposite short end of the piece of fabric, turn 6 cm (2¼ in) to the wrong side and press the fold.

6 Fold the piece of fabric in half with the wrong sides together and the short ends aligned so the flap is enclosed. Pin the sides together, and then tack along each side. Remove pins.

8 Turn the pillowcase inside out and tack along each side as for a French seam. Machine stitch and remove tacking.

9 Turn the pillowcase right side out and press it to finish.

7 Machine stitch through all layers along each side 6 mm ($\frac{1}{4}$ in) from the raw edges. Remove tacking and trim side seams to 3 mm ($\frac{1}{8}$ in).

Make a plain pillowcase in a bright primary colour or soft pastel shade to tone in with a leading colour in the bed linen. Or choose a smart striped material for the pillowcase, curtains and cushions to co-ordinate with plain bed linen.

FRILLED PILLOWCASE

If you want to add a co-ordinating or contrasting frill to a pillowcase, this method, which consists of three pieces of fabric, is best.

CHECK LIST

Materials

polyester/cotton sheeting – see Measuring up	
general sewing equipment	page 134

Techniques

cutting	page 136
tailor's tacks	page 138
machine stitching	page 140
making a frill	page 150
zigzag stitch	page 141
pressing	page 137

Measuring up

The pillowcase is made up of three sections as follows:

Front – Measure the length from A to B and the width from C to D. Add 3 cm (1¼ in) to each measurement.

Back – Add 4.5 cm (1⅞ in) to the length and 3 cm (1¼ in) to the width measurements.

Flap – Length is 17.5 cm (7 in). Measure width from C to D and add 3 cm (1¼ in). Width C to D plus 3 cm (1¼ in).

Frill – Strips of fabric 7.5 cm (3 in) wide and joined to equal 1½ times the perimeter of the pillow.

1 Lay the fabric right side down and mark out the cutting lines for the front, back, flap and frill pieces on it with tailor's chalk, based on your measurements. Cut out the pieces.

2 Find the centre on each side of the front piece and mark with tailor's tacks.

3 Join strips to make the frill, mark into four equal lengths with tailor's tacks and apply it to the front piece of the pillowcase, matching the tailor's tacks. Tack down the corners of the frill to the front piece.

4 Make a double hem on one long side of the flap piece by turning 6 mm (¼ in) to the wrong side twice, and pin in place. Tack the hem, remove the pins and machine stitch close to the tacking.

5 Place the flap piece over one end of the front piece with the right sides together and the raw edges aligned. Pin in place.

6 Tack the flap and front pieces together across the end. Remove the pins. Machine stitch through all layers close to the tacking.

7 Make a double hem across one of the short ends of the back piece by turning 1.5 cm ($\frac{5}{8}$ in) to the wrong side twice, and pin in place. Tack the hem, remove the pins, and machine stitch close to the tacking.

8 Open out the flap. Place the back piece over the front piece with the right sides together, and with the hemmed end of the back aligned with the flap seam. Pin in place, and then tack through all layers. Remove the pins.

9 Replace the flap over the back piece. Tack through all the layers of fabric along both long sides of the pillowcase and across the end opposite the flap.

10 Turn the assembled pillowcase over, and, following the frill stitching line, machine stitch 1.5 cm ($\frac{5}{8}$ in) in from the raw edges along both long sides and across the end opposite the flap.

11 Work a second row of machine stitching on the outside of the first row 6 mm ($\frac{1}{4}$ in) away from it, round all four sides. Trim the seam close to the stitching and neaten with a zigzag stitch.

12 Turn the pillowcase right side out. Remove the tacking stitches from the flap end and in the corners to release the frill, and press the pillowcase to finish.

Frilled pillowcases help to give a romantic look to a bedroom. The frill can be the same colour as the main pillow fabric, or choose a frill in a contrasting colour which echoes the fabric used for the curtains, bed valance or duvet cover.

DUVET COVER

Duvet covers are very easy to make because they are made from just two pieces of fabric sewn together. You could use the same fabric for both sides, or choose two contrasting fabrics, for a reversible duvet. Poppa-tape is used to close the opening at the bottom.

C H E C K L I S T

Materials

polyester/cotton sheeting – see Measuring up
general sewing equipment   page 134
poppa-tape 61 cm (24 in) shorter than the width of the duvet

Techniques

cutting   page 136
tacking   page 138
machine stitching   page 140
pressing   page 136

Measuring up

Following the diagram, measure the length of the duvet from A to B and add 6.5 cm (2⅝ in) for turnings, then double this measurement. Measure the width from C to D and add 3 cm (1¼ in) for seams.

Selvedge

Selvedge

1 Lay the fabric right side down and mark out the cutting lines for the two pieces of fabric with tailor's chalk. Cut out the two pieces.

2 Make a double hem across one end of each piece by turning 2.5 cm (1 in) to the wrong side twice, and pin in place. Tack the hem and remove the pins. Machine stitch close to the tacking, and then press the hems.

4 Tack along each line of pins, and then remove the pins. Machine stitch close to the tacking.

3 Place the two pieces of fabric with the right sides together and the hemmed edges aligned. Pin the two pieces together on the inside edge of the hem stitching at a distance of 30 cm (12 in) in from each side.

5 Unfasten the strip of poppa-tape and position each part with one long edge close to the hem stitching line across the opening. Check that the press studs will match for fastening and centre the tape so that a press stud is an equal distance from each side of the opening.

6 Machine stitch the tape in place using a zipper foot so that you can stitch in a straight line past the press studs. Fasten press studs.

9 Turn the cover inside out and machine stitch round the three sides 6 mm (¼ in) in from folded edges, enclosing the raw edges.

10 Turn the cover right sides out again and press. As an alternative fastening for the duvet cover, you could use buttons or tied bows.

7 At each end of opening, machine stitch down the hem from the folded edge to the stitching line to enclose the raw edges of the poppa-tape. Run a second line of the stitching close to the first and fasten off securely.

A reversible duvet cover is the easiest way to create a fully co-ordinated look that can mix and match with existing furnishings. Each side could be the same pattern in toning colours, or choose two differently-patterned fabrics in complementary colours.

8 Turn the cover right sides out. Pin down both the sides and top of the cover, then tack and remove the pins. Machine stitch 6 mm (¼ in) from the raw edges. Trim the seam to 3 mm (⅛ in).

BED VALANCE

A bed valance covers the bed base neatly, and can co-ordinate either with the bedding or with other furnishings in the room such as curtains. If this is your first attempt at making a large item, choose easy-to-handle sheeting for your fabric.

C H E C K L I S T

Materials

fabric – see Measuring up	
general sewing equipment	page 134
small plate	

Techniques

cutting	page 136
French seam	page 143
tacking	page 138
machine stitching	page 140
pressing	page 137
tailor's tacks	page 138

Measuring up

Main panel – measure the length from A to B and add 3.5 cm (1⅜ in) for turnings. Measure the width from C to D and add 3 cm (1¼ in).
Valance – measure the depth from E to F and add 2.5 cm (1 in). For the length, calculate 3 times the length (A to B) plus 1½ times the width (C to D). Add 4 cm (1½ in).

1 Based on the measurements of the bed, lay the fabric right side down and mark the cutting lines for the pieces required with tailor's chalk.

2 Cut out the main panel. Form a curve on each of the bottom corners by placing a small plate across the corner and drawing round it with tailor's chalk.

3 Cut out the fabric strips to make the required length for the valance, and join them into one continuous strip with French seams.

4 Make a double hem along one long edge of the valance strip by turning 1 cm (⅜ in) to the wrong side twice. Pin in place, tack the hem and remove pins. Machine stitch close to the tacking. Press the hem.

5 Divide the valance strip into six equal sections using a tape-measure, or by folding the valance. Mark the divisions with tailor's tacks.

6 With the right side up, work two rows of machining along the raw edge 1.5 cm ($\frac{5}{8}$ in) and 1 cm ($\frac{3}{8}$ in) from the edge. Use the longest stitch setting, and break off thread at each tailor's tack.

7 Divide the main panel into six equal sections around the sides and bottom edge, and mark with tailor tacks. Gather the valance and with right sides facing pin and tack it to the main panel, as for a frill.

8 Machine stitch the valance to the main panel 1.5 cm ($\frac{5}{8}$ in) in from the raw edges. Work another row of machine stitching using the second row of gathering as a guide.

9 Trim the seam close to the second row of stitching and stitch with a zigzag stitch to neaten. Press the seam towards the main panel.

10 Make a double hem across the straight end of the valance strip and the main panel by turning 1 cm ($\frac{3}{8}$ in) to the wrong side twice, and pin in place.

A gathered bed valance hides the base of the bed and can be made in a pretty fabric that co-ordinates with a frilled pillowcase or duvet cover. For a more striking look, use a bold, plain fabric that matches the sheets or duvet.

11 Tack across the top hem, remove the pins and machine stitch close to the tacking.

12 Press the valance to finish and spread over the bed base with the frilled short edge at the foot of the bed.

THROW-OVER BEDSPREAD

A throw-over bedspread covers all the bedding and is the best way to co-ordinate a bedroom, especially if it matches the curtains. This throw-over is reversible.

CHECK LIST

Materials

two co-ordinating fabrics – see Measuring up	
general sewing equipment	page 134
pencil	
string	

Techniques

cutting	page 136
pressing	page 137
tacking	page 138
machine stitching	page 140
slipstitch	page 139

Measuring up

Following the diagram, measure the bed (fully made up), to calculate the size of a floor-length bedspread. You will need equal amounts of the main fabric and the contrasting lining fabric. Measure the length from A to B, and add 25 cm (10 in) to allow for tucking in under the pillows. Measure the width from C to D. Add 9 cm (3¾ in) for seam allowances when the fabric is joined.

1 Lay one fabric right side down and mark out the cutting lines for the two lengths required based on the measurements of the bed. Make sure that any pattern is matching. Cut out the two pieces.

2 Trim the selvedge edges from the sides of both lengths, and cut one length in half lengthways. Place the half-widths one on each side of the full width, matching the pattern if necessary.

3 Place the full width and one half-width right sides together and pin down the long edge. Tack pieces together, remove the pins and machine stitch 1.5 cm (⅝ in) from the raw edges. Repeat on the other side.

4 To round off the corners at the bottom of the bedspread, measure the overhang from the top of the bed to the floor (E to F) and add 1.5 cm (⅝ in). Using the measurement, mark a square in each corner with tailor's chalk.

5 Take a pencil tied to a piece of string and hold the string on the inner corner of the square. Using one side of the square as the radius, draw an arc across the corner. Repeat on the other corner.

6 Cut off the bottom two corners of the bedspread carefully along the curved pencil line. Repeat instructions 2–7 to prepare the second fabric. Press all seams open.

9 Trim the seams and top corners. Snip 'V's out of the curved corners. Remove all the tacking.

11 With the tacking still in place, stitch round the edge of the bedspread using a medium to long machine stitch.

7 Lay the prepared fabrics right sides together, aligning the seams and raw edges. Pin and then tack the seams and edges together.

10 Turn the bedspread right side out and slipstitch across the opening to close it. Tack all round the edge of the bedspread, making sure that the seam is right on the edge and press.

12 Remove the tacking and give the bedspread a final press.

8 Machine stitch round the outside edges, leaving an opening of 90 cm (36 in) along the top.

A throw-over cover is quick and easy to make and adds instant focus to the bedroom. For a strong statement use a bold, ethnic design in vivid colours. For a softer look use a flowered fabric that contrasts with plain bed linen.

TABLE LINEN

Colour co-ordinated table linen made to match china as well as furnishings and decor creates an impressive and harmonious dining room setting. This section gives easy step-by-step instructions on how to make all the items required for a complete table arrangement: napkins, placemats and a bread roll holder. As table linen is so quick and easy, you can make a suitable setting for any occasion, from a children's birthday party using a bright and lively fabric, to a wedding reception requiring a fine damask material.

RECTANGULAR TABLECLOTH

From a children's party to a wedding anniversary, the perfect table setting begins with the tablecloth. This rectangular cloth, which has a hem corded with crochet cotton, is easy to make and can be used to match existing furnishings.

C H E C K   L I S T

Materials

fabric see Measuring up
crochet cotton
general sewing equipment   page 134

Techniques

cutting	page 136
pressing	page 137
mitring	page 144
zigzag stitch	page 141

Measuring up

Following the diagram, measure the table to calculate the amount of fabric required. Measure from A to B and then C to D. Add 50 cm (20 in) to both measurements to allow for overhang and hem allowance.

1 Lay the fabric right side down and mark the cutting lines for the size required with tailor's chalk, based on your measurements. Cut out the fabric.

2 Turn under a hem of 2.5 cm (1 in) to the wrong side on all four edges of the fabric and pin it in place. Press the hem and remove the pins.

3 Turn in a further 2.5 cm (1 in) to form a double hem and pin in place. Press the hem again.

4 Mitre the corners. Tack the hem in place, and then machine stitch close to the tacking.

5 With right side up, lay a single strand of crochet cotton over the hem stitching. Using a zigzag stitch and matching thread, machine over the cotton to form a corded hem, butting ends together where they join.

6 Press the tablecloth. To make co-ordinating placemats and napkins, see the box.

PLACEMATS AND NAPKINS

Rectangular placemats can be made using the same method as for the tablecloth. A piece of fabric 34 cm (13½ in) × 49 cm (19½ in) will give a finished size of 30 cm (12 in) × 45 cm (18 in) if a double turn of 1 cm (⅜ in) is used for the hems.

Napkins are generally square and range in size from 30 cm (12 in) for afternoon tea, to 60 cm (24 in) for a formal dinner. The average size for general use is usually between 45 cm (18 in) and 50 cm (20 in) square.

Matching placemats and napkins can be made to co-ordinate with a tablecloth or can be made in a contrasting fabric to add interest. Buy extra fabric when making the kitchen or dining room curtains to achieve a truly co-ordinated room and table.

ROUND TABLECLOTH

For small round side tables make a floor-length tablecloth with a shorter cloth over it. For a dining-table, the cloth should be lap height. If the fabric needs joining to fit a large table, stitch equal-size strips to each side of a full-width central panel.

CHECKLIST

Materials

paper for pattern
fabric see Measuring up
general sewing equipment   **page 134**

Techniques

patterns	**page 154**
cutting out	**page 136**
machine stitching	**page 140**
tacking	**page 138**
pressing	**page 137**

Measuring up

Following the diagram, measure the table to calculate the amount of fabric required. Measure the diameter from A to B and the depth of the required overhang from C to D. Double the overhang measurement and add 2 cm (¾ in) hem allowance to give the size for a square of fabric.

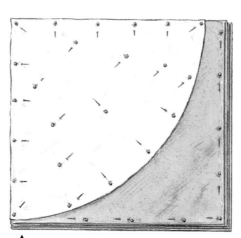

1 Fold the fabric in four and pin to secure the layers. Cut a piece of paper the same size as the folded fabric with an arc drawn across a corner to form a circle. Pin this pattern to the fabric and cut through all layers.

2 Machine stitch all round the circle of fabric, 1.5 cm (⅝ in) from the raw edge. Using the stitching line as a guide, press the edge of the fabric to the wrong side.

3 Turn under the raw edge to the pressed fold line to make a double hem and pin in place. Tack down the hem, remove pins and then press.

4 Machine stitch all round the hem on the fold line and press it again. The double pressing helps to give a professional finish.

5 For a stylish finish, add a contrasting or co-ordinating over-lay. A lace over-lay on a plain coloured fabric adds an attractive touch.

OVER-LAY

To make a round over-lay for the tablecloth, follow the same instructions, measuring a depth of about one third of the top-to-floor measurement. This will be easier to judge if you make the full-length cloth first.

QUILTED PLACEMATS

Quilted placemats, which consist of a layer of wadding covered with fabric can be made to co-ordinate with the rest of the table linen. To quilt the mat, rows of stitching are machined or hand sewn through all the layers.

CHECKLIST

Materials (for each placemat)

paper for pattern
1 piece each of 2 co-ordinating fabrics – 45 cm
  (18 in) × 30 cm (12 in)
1 piece medium-weight wadding 45 cm
  (18 in) × 30 cm (12 in)
approximately 1.40 m (1⅝ yd) of 2.5 cm (1 in) wide
  bias binding (or make your own see page 148)
general sewing equipment   page 134

Techniques

cutting	page 136
tacking	page 138
machine stitching	page 140
slipstitch	page 139

Making the pattern

Fold a piece of paper measuring 45 cm (18 in) by 30 cm (12 in) into four. Mark with pencil 15 cm (6 in) in from point A, and draw an arc to make an oval. Cut out the pattern.

1 For each placemat cut out one piece of each co-ordinating fabric and one piece of wadding using the paper pattern.

2 Place the wadding to the wrong side of the contrast fabric, and lay the main fabric right side up over the wadding.

3 Tack the three layers together, working from the centre outwards. Machine stitch the layers together using a large stitch setting, either following a design on the fabric or working freehand without creating any particular design.

4 Fold over 1 cm (⅜ in) to the wrong side of one end of the bias binding. Place the bias binding right side down on the right side of the main fabric, with raw edges even and pin in place.

5 Tack the bias binding in place and remove the pins. Machine stitch 1 cm (⅜ in) from the raw edges. Fold the bias binding over to the contrast fabric side. Slipstitch it neatly along the machine stitching and at the join.

6 Lightly press the binding, but do not press the quilting.

BREAD-ROLL HOLDER

A bread-roll holder that matches the tablecloth or napkins provides an attractive centrepiece. This one is made from three circles of fabric laid on top of each other with matching ribbons for ties.

C H E C K L I S T

Materials

paper for pattern	
50 cm (20 in) of 2 co-ordinating fabrics	
50 cm (20 in) iron-on interfacing	
3 m (3½ yds) cotton lace trim	
2 m of 3 mm (⅛ in) wide ribbon	
general sewing equipment	page 134

Techniques

cutting	page 136
pressing	page 137
tacking	page 138
machine stitching	page 140
slipstitch	page 139
zigzag stitch	page 141

Making the pattern

Make a pattern by folding a 30 cm (12 in) square piece of paper into four. Draw an arc across a corner to make a circle and cut out the pattern. Divide it into twelve equal segments and mark them in pencil.

1 Cut out three circles from each fabric, and three from the interfacing, using the paper pattern. Position the pieces of interfacing on the wrong sides of the main fabric circles and press in place.

2 Pin the lace trim to the right sides all around the edges of the main fabric circles. Tack the lace trim in place, remove the pins and machine stitch in place.

3 Place the contrast fabric circles over the trimmed circles with right sides facing, and pin them together.

4 Tack all round 1 cm (⅜ in) from the raw edges, and remove the pins. Machine stitch following the stitching from applying the lace, leaving a 10 cm (4 in) opening for turning right side out.

5 Trim the seams and snip out small 'V's all round the edge of each circle. Turn right sides out and slipstitch the gap closed. Press each circle.

6 Place the paper pattern onto the contrast side of one of the circles and transfer every other line, to give six segments, using tailor's chalk.

7 Cut the ribbon into three equal pieces. Centre them over the chalk lines and stitch them down with zigzag stitch. Place the pattern over this circle again, and mark the lines between the ribbons.

10 Turn the joined circles over, and place the third circle, with the contrast fabric uppermost, on top. Mark lines from the points where the ribbons meet the edge of the circle, towards the centre, with tailor's chalk.

12 Machine stitch on the tack lines, working with the middle circle uppermost and from the outer edge of the circle towards the centre.

8 Place the circle with the ribbons uppermost over the main fabric side of a second circle. Pin them together along the chalk lines, working from the centre outwards. Tack along the lines and remove the pins.

11 Pin along the lines for 7.5 cm (3 in) through the top and middle circles *only*. Tack along the lines and remove the pins.

13 Bring the opposite ribbons together and tie them in bows. Insert the bread roll holder into a basket and open out pockets.

9 Machine stitch close to the tacking, starting at the centre for each line of stitching and working outwards. Remove tacking.

A bread roll holder is not only an eye-catching alternative to a bread basket, but it is a practical way of helping to harmonise a table setting. Choose from a wide range of lace trims.

TECHNIQUES

The techniques used in this book are all quite straightforward and are shown here in step-by-step detail. There is also information on equipment, how to alter curtains for windows if dimensions differ from the size for which they were originally intended, and how to enlarge and reduce patterns. When trying a sewing technique for the first time, it is advisable to have a test run on a spare piece of fabric if possible.

EQUIPMENT

WHEN BUILDING up your work basket, if possible buy good quality sewing equipment as more expensive items will far outlast cheaper makes. Scissors are the most costly items and more than one pair is needed as different sizes are required for different tasks, but a good quality pair should last a lifetime.

Some projects in this book require specialist items that need only be bought if necessary. But for ease of work and professional results, your sewing basket should contain the following general equipment.

1 Sewing and knitting gauge
2 Pins
3 Cutting-out shears
4 Pinking shears (optional)
5 Tape measure
6 Decorator's steel ruler
7 Tacking cotton
8 Fabric pens/pencils
9 Machine needles
10 Small scissors
11 Thimble
12 Tailor's chalk
13 Hand sewing needles
14 Metre/Yard stick

Cutting-out shears: 20 cm (8 in) or 23 cm (9 in) side-bent to give a comfortable hold, made from forged steel, they can be sharpened and adjusted.

Small scissors: which are sharp right to the point, used for snipping and trimming.

A decorators' steel tape: would be an invaluable extra for measuring windows for curtains etc.

Sewing and knitting gauge: a small metal ruler, having an adjustable slide marker.

Medium-size scissors: 15 cm (6 in) for cutting out the paper patterns.

Tape measure: obtain a fibre glass one which will not stretch.

Metre/Yard stick: for marking long lines either on paper or fabric.

Tailor's chalk: a special chalk for use on fabric, either in tablet or pencil form, available in various colours.

Fabric pens/pencils: for quick marking. Some just fade away, others are removed by water. Always test on the fabric being used.

Pins: dressmakers' steel pins with highly polished points will prevent snagging fabrics. Several specialized ones are also available. Extra fine steel pins 30 mm ($1\frac{3}{16}$ in) long are recommended.

Hand sewing needles: an assorted pack gives a selection of lengths and sizes suitable for most fabrics.

Machine needles: have a selection of types and sizes, purchasing the system that your sewing machine and overlocker manual advises.

Tacking cotton: absolutely essential for all tacking. It is a soft thread which easily breaks, avoiding harming fabric as it is being pulled out.

Thimble: should be worn for all hand sewing, including tacking, very necessary when working with thicker fabrics.

Sewing machine: gives a strong stitch that withstands the everyday wear and tear of many items. Your machine should be able to produce a straight stitch in different lengths and zigzag stitch in various widths.

PRESSING
For professional pressing the following is required:
Steam iron (used dry)
Terry towels
Butter muslin cloth
Ironing board: preferably with felt underlay and cotton cover.

Non-essential items
Non-essential items that are very useful when making certain projects, include the following:

Bodkin: a thick, blunt, round or flat needle with a large eye for threading elastic or tape into hems or casings.

Thread snips: for cutting thread only (having these prevents blunting the small scissors).

Rouleau turner: a long thick needle, sometimes with a ball end which can be pushed into a sewn bias strip. The eye is sewn to the fabric before going right into the strip to turn it right side out.

Overlocker/serger: machine that trims, sews and neatens in one operation very quickly.

Trimming and tape maker: a most useful easy to use gadget for making your own binding. Strips of fabric, cut on the bias, are fed through the tape maker and as they are pulled through, the sides of the bias are folded, ready to be pressed with the iron.

Pattern paper: special paper printed with squares for scaling up diagram patterns on a grid system.

Flexible curve: this can be shaped to follow any line.

Cutting board: made from cardboard, it folds for easy storage and is printed with squares generally 2.5 cm (1 in). It can be used for cutting out, calculating fabric and making patterns from a diagram.

WORKING WITH FABRIC

MOST FURNISHING fabrics are made in the following widths, 122 cm (48 in), 137 cm (54 in) and 152 cm (60 in) and are rolled on cardboard tubes by the manufacturer, but some, and lining materials, are folded, and then are wound onto a rectangular piece of composite board. A ticket should give the fabric content, care instructions, and where appropriate, the pattern repeat measurement.

When buying fabric it is always advisable to buy a little bit extra to allow for uneven cutting.

The descriptive terms used for fabric will soon become familiar.

• The *selvedge* is the firm woven edge of fabric, it should not be used but trimmed away.
• The *straight grain* is parallel to the selvedge, and it is important that the cut ends, which are across the width of the fabric, are straightened before cutting lengths.
• The *bias* is a diagonal line across the weave of the fabric. To find the true bias; measure the same distance along the selvedge and the cut edge, having first made sure the latter is at right angles to the selvedge, mark the points measured and draw a line using tailor's chalk and a metre/yard stick.
• The *crosswise grain* runs from selvedge to selvedge.

Cutting fabric

▲ All fabric should be cut on the straight grain, that is where the warp (the lengthwise thread parallel to the selvedge) is at right angles to the weft (the crosswise thread). Therefore, before cutting lengths it will be necessary to straighten the cut edge. To do this snip into the selvedge and pull out a thread, if the weave is loose enough; alternatively, use a set square and mark a line with tailor's chalk. Cut across the fabric on the resulting line.
• When cutting out fabric place the left hand lightly onto the fabric to the left of the pattern or marked line and the scissors held in the right hand ready to cut, having the pattern or marked line to the right of the scissors. Reverse left and right if you are left-handed.
• Cut all lengths in the same direction. With some fabrics, the direction of the design is obvious, as the word 'TOP' is actually printed on the selvedge. Other fabrics, even plain ones, have to be scrutinised, as they could have a sheen which affects their appearance when viewed in different lights. Velvets, for example, can appear darker or lighter when viewed in a hanging position – when used with the pile running upwards, they seem richer in colour, and lighter with the pile running downwards.

Joining fabric

• Blinds require a join with an open seam placed as unobtrusively as possible. Roman blinds are better made without a seam, but if it cannot be avoided an equal amount either side of a central panel could be added and a flat trim machined over the seam on the right side can look attractive. Balloon blinds can have a seam placed under a pleat and Austrian blinds where a line of rings will be creating ruching.

▲ When making large items, fabric has to be joined to attain the necessary width. Each curtain can require 1½/2/2½ widths and any half width is placed to the sides furthest away from the centre, where the curtains meet when closed. Unlined curtains are better joined with a run and fell seam and lined curtains with an open seam.

▲ Bedspreads and tablecloths have an equal amount added to each side of a full width, both can be joined with open seams and the raw edges neatened.

Bias line

Straight grain

▲ Extra material needed for a swag is joined on the straight grain with an open seam before the swag is cut out. The seam would be positioned in the bottom corner and would be hidden within the pleats when made.

Pinning fabric

Place pins diagonally when pinning a pattern to fabric ready for cutting out and well within the edges, only a few pins are necessary. The exception to this "rule" is when working with a fabric that pin marks, then place the pins within the seam allowance.

• When pinning two layers of fabric together place pins raw edges inwards, this prevents pushing one layer of fabric ahead of the other. The exception to this tip is when you have piping on one layer then the pins have to go along the seam.

Pressing fabric

• Always have the iron and ironing board ready to press at each stage, and when pressing large items have your ironing board alongside a table in order to take the weight of the item.

• Make sure the iron setting is right for the type of fabric, and always test press a piece before beginning your project.

• Pressing cloths are needed, and several types are available; using butter muslin has the added advantage that you can see through it and therefore position your iron correctly. Buy 1 m (1 yd) of muslin and cut it in half to provide two pressing cloths; one to use damp and the other dry. To make a cloth damp soak it in water and wring out firmly. This is adequate for light/medium fabrics but fold it double for thicker materials.

• Use the iron with an up-and-down action rather than sliding it along as when ironing laundry.

• To press seams, first, press along the seam with layers of fabric together as sewn and covered with a damp muslin cloth. Then press the seam open, using your fingers and the point of the iron to open the seam. A final press with a damp cloth is required. If the fabric is thick tuck pieces of the same fabric under each side of the open seam. It is sometimes necessary to place a dry cloth over the seam and re-press.

• A seam that is on the edge of an item, e.g. self-bordered square cushion, requires preparation before pressing. After turning right side out roll the seam between fingers and thumbs to bring it to the edge, tack as you go along. Press well, using a damp cloth, warm/hot iron and medium pressure with the side of the iron just over the edge of the seam.

• There are a few fabrics that require dry pressing only. For these always place a dry pressing cloth over the fabric to prevent any damage to it and experiment with spare material if you are doubtful.

• Placing a terry towel on the ironing board prevents raised textured fabrics being flattened when pressed.

• Velvet can be pressed on another piece of velvet placed right side uppermost but ideally on a needleboard.

HAND STITCHING

When hand sewing, especially on dark fabrics, work in natural light if possible, although daylight bulbs are now available and well worth purchasing. Choose matching thread suitable for the fabric for any permanent stitching, synthetic for man-made fabrics and cotton for material made from natural fibres. For temporary and marking stitches use tacking cotton, which is a special soft thread made for the purpose which will not damage fabric when being taken out. Do not work with a long piece of thread; the length of your arm is quite sufficient. Cutting, not breaking, the thread from the reel, makes threading a needle easier.

Needles need to be appropriate for the fabric and thread; fine needles pierce the fabric more easily, and you are less likely to snag or pull a thread in the weave. Packets of mixed needles include various sizes and lengths from which to select.

There is some hand sewing on nearly everything that is made from fabric, possibly only tacking, which is merely a temporary stitch until a permanent machine stitch has been worked. Hand sewing of curtain hems is, in most cases, preferable, as the stitches are worked so that they are invisible from the right side. When sewing hems, have the bulk of the curtain on a table with the hem towards you, this way the weight is well supported and the curtain will not get so creased.

A thimble should be worn on the middle finger of your sewing hand for protection, especially when sewing thicker or firmly woven materials.

Tacking

A temporary stitch used to hold two pieces of fabric together while further processes are worked. The length of the stitches needs to be made in relation to the fabric; fine material would require a smaller stitch, while for a fabric that is thicker, and unlikely to slip, a larger stitch would be adequate. If you do find you have pulled the stitches tightly do not retack but just snip the thread to release the tension every now and again along the length of the seam before machining. Always remove pins as you tack.

Using tacking cotton, knot one end to secure the thread in the material when making the first stitch. Do not work more than two stitches at a time before pulling the needle through, and do *not* pull the thread tightly otherwise the fabric will pucker. To finish, fasten the cotton with a back stitch and cut the thread leaving a 5 cm (2 in) end.

Tailor's tacks

Tailor's tacks are worked using double tacking cotton without a knot on the end and are used to mark a certain point for matching up with another piece of fabric.

Make a stitch 6mm ($\frac{1}{4}$ in) and leave the ends 1 cm ($\frac{3}{8}$ in), make another stitch over the first leaving a loop 2 cm ($\frac{3}{4}$ in), repeat to make a second loop and cut the threads leaving the ends 1 cm ($\frac{3}{8}$ in).

Back stitch

A secure stitch used for short runs and worked from right to left. Use thread with a knot on the end.

Bring the needle up through the fabric from the back, a little way from the beginning to allow the needle to be placed back to the beginning and down through the fabric, then the needle is brought up ahead of the first stitch. Continue in this way until the end, when two back stitches are worked on the spot.

Ladder stitch

Ladder stitch (sometimes called sliptacking) is also a tacking stitch. It is used when matching a pattern in joining two pieces of material, and it is worked from the right.

Press under the seam allowance on one side, taking care not to stretch the fabric. Place the folded edge over the seam allowance matching the pattern exactly and pin firmly in place. Knot the thread under the folded edge and bring the needle up to the right side. Move the needle across the fold and take a stitch in line with the folded edge. Pull through and take a stitch across the folded edge again, between the two layers of fabric. Take a stitch of 2 cm ($\frac{3}{4}$ in) and bring the needle back through to the right side.

Blanket stitch

Blanket stitch can be used to neaten raw edges securely or attach curtain rings, to a tie-back for example.

Fasten the thread under the raw edge of the fabric and bring the needle through to the right side. With the needle held at right angles, loop the thread behind the point. Pull through and continue with even stitches and the thread loops lying neatly along the edge.

Slipstitch

A stitch that is very nearly invisible on both sides of the fabric when used on a hemline or any other folded edge.

Secure the end of the thread with a couple of stitches inside the folded edge, then slide the needle along the fold of the hem for 5 mm ($\frac{1}{4}$ in) and pull through. With the point of the needle, pick up a few threads from the fabric exactly opposite, pull through and insert into the fold again. Continue in this way, taking care not to pull the thread too tightly. When using this stitch for mitred corners, slide the needle along both folds, first on one side then the other.

Catchstitch

A stitch to join two layers of fabric loosely together, worked slightly under one fabric, making an invisible join. This is an ideal stitch to attach a detachable lining to a curtain.

Fold back the lining and take a small stitch in the side hem, then a stitch in the curtain. Work further stitches first on one side then the other. Do not pull the thread tightly.

Lockstitch

Lockstitch is used in curtain-making to anchor lining and interlining to curtain fabric. It is worked with the fabric and lining placed with wrong sides together.

Pin the centres together down the complete length and fold the lining back. Make two or three stitches in the fold of the lining near the top. Then, working downwards and keeping the thread loose, pick up a couple of threads from the fabric and the lining. The needle goes over the thread to "lock" it, and the stitches need to be approximately 10–15 cm (4–6 in) apart.

Herringbone stitch

Herringbone stitch is worked from left to right and is a securing stitch. The stitches should not be worked too tightly as this allows them to be seen from the right side.

Fasten the thread with a couple of stitches and bring the needle up through the hem. Move it diagonally to the right just above the hem, and pick up a few threads from the fabric. With the needle moved further to the right, take a stitch in the hem. The needle is held horizontal throughout and the thread is kept below it.

Machine Stitching

Machine sewing produces a strong permanent stitch that will withstand the test of time and the use of the item. A manual comes with every sewing machine and should be studied for the various features and explanations on the tension and setting of the length for straight stitch, width for zigzag stitch etc.

Always test the stitch on a double layer of spare fabric that is going to be used for a project, selecting the needle, thread and stitch length that are appropriate.

Remember to change the needle frequently, after about eight to twelve hours' sewing, and make sure you are using the correct type and size for the fabric and thread. Failing to do this will result in skipped and badly formed stitches.

If your sewing machine does not seem to be sewing correctly, first change the needle, and if there is no improvement check the threading both of the top and bottom. The bobbin thread has to wind off in a certain way – clockwise or anti-clockwise – your manual should either say or make it clear with illustrations.

If the table you are using for machine sewing is not large enough to hold the material, place an adjustable ironing board at table-top height to the left of the table and use this to support the material. Alternatively, place three or four chairs with their backs against the table and drape the material over the chair backs with the material resting on the seats.

If you are machining with the seam just pinned, always remove the pins as you are machining.

Using a machine

1 When starting to machine hold the top and bottom threads together towards the back, thus preventing them from tangling underneath.

2 Your machine will feed the material under the pressure foot, without any need to push it from the front or pull it from the back. If you do either, it will result in uneven stitching. Light finger tip control to guide the fabric on the stitching line is all that is required.

Straight stitch

This stitch is used in varying lengths and needs to be adjusted for different fabrics, the stitch is equally strong whether small or large. It is the stitch most used for seams. Always make the first test run with a medium length stitch setting on a double layer of material.

Edge stitch

A straight stitch worked on the right side very near to the edge of the fabric.

Top stitch

A straight stitch worked with the right side of the fabric uppermost, normally 6 mm (¼ in) from the edge unless a specific measurement is given.

Zigzag stitch

This is used for neatening seams, and is ideal on frequently laundered items such as bed linen. Trimmings such as ribbons and flat braids look better when sewn on with zigzag stitch. Use it also to sew touch-and-close fastener tape.

Gathering on medium and thick materials can be made easier by machining over a thin cord with zigzag stitch.

OVERLOCKING

An overlocker/serger trims, sews and neatens a seam in one operation, at twice the speed of a conventional sewing machine. A three-thread stitch using one upper sewing thread, in either the left or the right needle (it depends on the fabric being sewn) and two loopers threaded with overlocking thread is ideal for neatening seams. A four-thread stitch; two upper sewing threads and two loopers threaded with overlocking thread, produces a strong seam suitable for bed linen items.

Three-thread stitch

Four-thread stitch

Gathering stitch

Set the machine to the longest straight stitch setting and reduce the top tension a little. Make a test run with a single or double layer of fabric, whichever is being used in the project. With the right side uppermost, work two rows of stitching, one just within the seam allowance and the other 6 mm (¼ in) from the first. Pull the bobbin threads together to form the gathers, distributing them evenly. If a long length of fabric needs to be gathered, divide the length in equal sections and break the thread between each.

SEAMS

THERE ARE many different ways of joining seams, and it is essential to sew the seam that is appropriate for the fabric and the item you are making. A plain, open seam is used for joining two pieces of fabric together. A double seam or French seam is used to enclose raw edges, especially on lightweight or sheer fabrics, and is a very hard-wearing seam. The run and fell seam, also a strong seam, gives a flatter finish than a French seam and is ideal for items that require frequent washing. Run and fell seams are suitable for unlined items such as kitchen or bathroom curtains. A flat, lapped seam is used to join interlining.

Open seam

1 Place the pieces of fabric right sides together and pin at right angles from the raw edges inwards. Tack just inside the seam line and remove pins.

3 Press the stitching into the fabric first, then open the seam flat and press the seam.

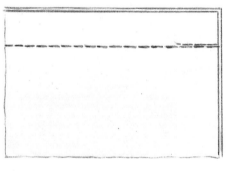

2 Machine stitch, using the normal seam allowance of 1.5 cm ($\frac{5}{8}$ in) unless otherwise stated. Work down the length of the item, ie, from the top of a curtain towards the hemline, and reverse the stitching for a short way at each end to secure the ends. Remove the tacking.

Lapped seam

1 With the right side of both pieces of fabric uppermost, overlap one piece over the other by 1.5 cm ($\frac{5}{8}$ in).

2 Machine with a large zigzag stitch to secure the raw edges, or sew by hand using herringbone stitch.

French seam

1 Place the pieces of the fabric wrong sides together and pin from the raw edges inwards. Tack just inside the seam line, if necessary. Machine stitch 9 mm ($\frac{3}{8}$ in) from the raw edges, and then trim the seam to 3mm ($\frac{1}{8}$ in). Remove the tacking.

2 Turn the fabric so that the right sides are together. Roll the seam between fingers and thumbs to bring it to the edge. If you moisten your fingers, it will help you to grip the fabric. Tack as you work along the seam, enclosing the raw edge of the first seam.

3 Press the seam. Then machine 6 mm ($\frac{1}{4}$ in) from the edge of the item, and press the seam again.

Run and fell seam

1 Place the pieces of fabric wrong sides together and pin. Tack the seam and then machine stitch 1.5 cm ($\frac{5}{8}$ in) from the raw edges. If you are using a thick fabric make the seam wider, having allowed for this when cutting out.

2 Press the seam open. Trim one side of the seam allowance only, down to 6 mm ($\frac{1}{4}$ in).

3 Press the seam to one side with the larger seam allowance on top.

4 Turn the larger seam allowance under 6 mm ($\frac{1}{4}$ in), tacking it down as you work along the seam.

5 Press the seam before and after machine stitching it to the fabric close to the edge. Do not press towelling.

MITRED CORNERS

A mitred corner gives a neat, flat appearance to the hems of curtains or table linen. How you make your mitre depends on what it is for. To form a mitre with the same turning on both sides of the corner, as for a tablecloth, use Method 1. To form a mitre with a single-turn side and a double-turn bottom hem, as for tube-lined and locked-in lined curtains, use Method 2. For single-turn side and bottom hems, for inter-lined and lined curtains, use Method 3.

Method One

1 Make a turning of 2.5 cm (1 in) on both sides of the corner and press in place.

2 Make a second turn of 2.5 cm (1 in) on both sides and press again.

3 Unfold the second turn and fold in the corner on the diagonal. Press the diagonal fold.

4 Unfold the diagonal and place the right sides of the fabric together. Machine stitch along the creaseline of the diagonal fold.

5 Trim the seam to 6 mm ($\frac{1}{4}$ in) and press it open.

6 Turn the corner right side out. Re-fold the hem and machine stitch in place.

Method Two

1 Press the single-turn side hem and the double-turn bottom hem. Unfold the side and the second turn of the bottom hem.

2 Press a diagonal fold, having twice the turning allowance of the side measurement along the bottom, and twice the turning allowance of the hem measurement along the side.

3 Refold and slipstitch in place. If the fabric is very thick, trim off the excess before refolding.

Method Three

1 Press the single turn side hem and the single turn bottom hem. Unfold the side and bottom hems. Proceed as steps 1 and 2, Method Two.

WEIGHTS

The addition of coin weights significantly improves the hanging of curtains and they can be added while mitring the corners. They should be sewn to the hem before stitching the mitre. Alternatively, a lead-weight tape available by the metre can be slotted along the full length of the hem. This requires catching at each end and in several places along the hemline.

FASTENERS

MANY SOFT furnishing items, such as cushion and duvet covers, can be fastened in different ways. Zips are neat and strong and are ideal on cushions, especially seat cushions. Touch-and-close fastener tape is most versatile, and there are two types that can be used when making soft furnishings; one is sewn to both sections, the other is a very efficient way of fixing pelmets or blinds to a pelmet board/shelf. The self-adhesive hook side is pressed into position on the board/shelf, and the loop side sewn in place to the pelmet or blind.

Fabric ties are another form of fastening, which add that personal touch and give a completely co-ordinated look. The length and width of a self-fabric tie depends on whether a simple knot or a bow is required and if the function is to pull two edges together, or if a cushion needs to be held in place by being tied to the back of the chair. It is a simple matter to position and pin a length of tape in place, tie a bow and then take a measurement. The finished width of the tie can be very narrow, 2 cm (¾ in), medium 5 cm (2 in) or 10 cm (4 in) wide, or even wider.

Fabric ties

1 Cut two strips of fabric on the straight grain, double the finished width plus 2 cm (¾ in) seam allowance by the length required.

2 Fold in half lengthways, pin and machine stitch with a 1 cm (⅜ in) seam, removing the pins as you machine. Push a large-eyed, long, blunt needle or bodkin into the tube and firmly stitch to one side of the tube.

3 Turn the strip right side out by working the needle/bodkin down the tube, ruching the fabric over, then easing it off until the strip is completely turned. Press well and neaten one end by hand. Insert the raw edge in a seam or turn the raw edge under and stitch in place.

4 For a wider tie leave a central opening on the long edge to enable the ends to be machine stitched. Turn right side out through the opening.

Touch-and-close

Touch-and-close consists of two pieces of tape-like material woven from nylon, one side having tiny soft loops and the other tiny firm hooks. Press them together and they make a very strong bond. Pull them apart to sew them in place where required with zigzag stitch, aligning one with the other to ensure they meet correctly for fastening.

Touch-and-close spots are small discs of the same type of material and are held in place with a triangle of hand or machine stitching.

Zips

 With the right sides of the fabric together, machine stitch the full length of the seam as follows: stitch the seams up to the zip opening with a normal-size stitch, and reverse to secure the stitching. Then stitch the zip opening with the largest size stitch. Press the seam open.

2 Tack guide lines on the right side of the fabric 6 mm ($\frac{1}{4}$ in) on both sides of the seam where the zip is to be positioned.

3 Position the closed zip, right side down, on the wrong side of the fabric over the seam line, centring the teeth. Pin to hold it while you are tacking it in place from the right side. Thread two needles with tacking cotton and tack along the two sides of the zip alternately.

4 Fit the zipper foot to the machine and stitch the zip in place on the right side. Start at the seam at the bottom of the zip and stitch across at right angles to the zip, pivoting the fabric round the needle when you reach the guide line. Continue machining, pausing with the needle in the fabric 7.5 cm (3 in) from the zip tab end.

5 Release the zipper foot and carefully take out some of the long machine stitches to enable the zip to be opened past the machine needle. Lower the presser foot and continue sewing to the end of the guide line. Pivot the fabric round the needle with the needle in the fabric and stitch to the seam line.

6 Machine stitch the other side of the zip in the same way. Be careful to stitch a straight line past the zip tab.

7 Remove the tacking and remaining long machine stitches. Knot the machine threads on the wrong side.

Poppa-snaps

A practical and decorative non-sew fastener with two parts to each section that fasten in place on either side of the fabric. They are sold in packs complete with full instructions and a hand tool to hold them in position until they are fixed.

Poppa-tape

Poppa-tape consists of two pieces of tape with poppas (press studs) attached at intervals along their length. Tapes are sewn on separately with a straight stitch using the zipper foot.

BINDING AND PIPING

BINDING RAW edges gives a quick neat finish. Use bias binding for a shaped item as this will go round corners easily as it has a certain amount of stretch. Straight binding is needed when a firm edge is required as for the swag and tails.

Piping gives a finishing touch to a cushion and can be made in a contrasting or coordinating colour to add interest. It also gives extra strength to seat cushions or anything that will be in constant use. Piping is made from strips of material cut on the bias with a piping cord inserted. Piping cord is made in different numbered sizes, with 3–5 being the most often used on soft furnishings. Always check that it is pre-shrunk.

QUICK BIAS BINDING

There is now a useful gadget on the market which forms folded edges on the side of the bias strip (see page 134). The bias strip is fed through a wide end and pulled through a narrow one, turning the edges which are pressed with an iron as they appear.

Continuous bias binding

1 Mark the bias at one side of the piece of fabric and cut off the end corner.

Move the triangular off-cut of fabric to the other side of the rectangle, and with right sides together, join them with a 6 mm (¼ in) open seam. Press the seam open.

2 On the wrong side of the piece of fabric mark cutting lines to the required width parallel to the ends. Mark a 6 mm (¼ in) seam allowance at the side. Mark with pins points A and B on the seamline as shown.

3 With the right sides facing, bring together the two pins at points A and B. Pin the sides together along the seamline to produce a tube with the width of a single strip protruding at each end of the seam.

4 Tack along the line of pins, and remove the pins. Machine stitch along the seam line, and press the seam open carefully. Cut along the marked lines to make one continuous strip of bias binding.

Applying a bias strip

1 Fold and press the binding in half. Holding the bias binding in the left hand, curve the binding to fit the item using a medium hot iron.

2 Insert the edges of the item between the folded bias binding. Pin, tack and zigzag in place, neatening the join of the binding by turning under one edge to overlap the other.

Straight binding

This is a strip of fabric preferably cut on the straight lengthways grain of material, but can be cut from the width of material on the crossways grain. Measurements for cutting the strips and applying them are given in the instructions for the individual items.

3 Lay the piping cord along the centre of the strip of fabric on the wrong side. Fold the fabric over the piping cord. Align the raw edges and pin the fabric near the cord. Tack along the line of pins, and remove the pins. With the zipper foot on the machine, stitch close to the cord. Remove tacking.

3 Cut across the piping on one end. On the other end pull back the bias strip and cut the cord only, ensuring that the ends butt together snugly. Turn the bias strip under across the free end to neaten it and cover the raw edge of the first end. Complete machining the piping on the seam line.

To make piping

1 Cut bias strips from the fabric 4–6 mm (1½–2⅜ in) wide, depending on the size of the cord. The strips should be wide enough to go round the cord and have a double seam allowance of 1.5 cm (⅝ in).

To apply piping

1 Place the piping to the right side of the first fabric piece. Align the raw edges and pin the piping to the fabric piece. Tack them together, snipping the curves or corners as you work, and leave an overlap of 2.5 cm (1 in) where the ends of the piping meet. Remove the pins.

4 Place the first and second pieces of fabric right sides together. Pin and tack them together, and remove the pins. Turn the work over so that you can follow the first line of stitching from applying the piping, and machine the seam, using the zipper foot.

2 Join the strips of fabric on the straight grain with 6 mm (¼ in) open seams, and press the seams open.

2 Machine the piping in place, starting 2.5 cm (1 in) from one end and stopping the same distance from the other end.

FRILLS AND PLEATS

FRILLS MADE from single and double fabric can be used to add an attractive trimming. Made in a contrasting colour they will give an added interest to many home furnishings and are an excellent way to co-ordinate the item with other focal points in a room.

A pleated trim can be used instead of a gathered frill. It is especially attractive for the bottom of a tie-back. The fabric required for a pleated trim is three times the measurement to be trimmed. Experiment with the fabric that is going to be used; smaller pleats can be formed on thin/medium materials, but thicker fabric will require larger pleats.

Single frill

A single frill can be any width that is in proportion with the item. The length of the piece of fabric should be at least 1½ times the measurement round the item, such as a pillowcase, to which it will be applied.

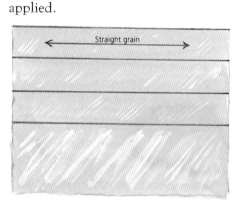

1 Cut out strips of fabric on the straight grain. Remember to add on a 1.5 cm (⅝ in) seam allowance and a double hem allowance of 1 to 2 cm (⅜ in–¾ in), depending on the thickness of the fabric.

2 Join the strips of fabric with run and fell seams into one continuous round. Turn up 6 mm (¼ in) twice to the wrong side all round the bottom edge of the frill and pin. Tack the hem and remove the pins. Machine stitch the hem.

3 Divide the frill into four sections and mark with pins. Machine two rows of gathering with the first row just inside the seam allowance and the other 6 mm (¼ in) above it. Break off the threads at each pin.

4 Divide the item to be trimmed into four sections and mark with pins. Pull up the bobbin threads on each section so that the sections match those on the item being trimmed.

5 With right sides together, place the frill to the item being trimmed, matching the division marks and aligning the raw edges. Adjust the gathers evenly and pin the frill in place. Tack the frill in place and remove the pins. Machine stitch.

6 Machine stitch again 6 mm (¼ in) above the first line of stitching. Trim the seam close to the stitching, and zigzag stitch along the seam to neaten it.

Straight double frill

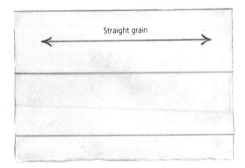

1 Cut strips 18 cm (7¼ in) wide by twice the bottom measurement of the item being trimmed, allowing extra for any seams that are necessary to make the required length.

2 Join the strips with an open seam and press. Fold in half lengthways right sides together and stitch the ends.

3 Turn right sides out and press. Divide into four and mark with tailor's tacks.

4 Machine two rows of gathering stitch making a break of threads at the tailor's tacks. The frill is now ready to apply (see Austrian Blind, step 3).

Round double frill

If the fabric for the frill is used double, the need for a hem is eliminated. To make a double frill, you will need twice the finished width of the frill plus a double seam allowance. For a finished 5 cm (2 in) frill with a seam allowance of 1.3 cm (½ in), cut strips on the straight grain 12.5 cm (5 in) wide by the length required.

Join the strips into a round with open seams, and press the seams open. Fold the fabric in half lengthways with the wrong sides together and then proceed as for the single frill.

Pleats

For 1.3 cm (½ in) pleats mark the raw edge with pins 1.3 cm (½ in)– 2.5 cm (1 in) apart all the way along. Follow the direction of the arrow on the illustration to form the pleats.

ADAPTING CURTAINS

THE PROVISION OF SETS of curtains for all the rooms in a new house can be a daunting task – and expensive. It may be possible to adapt existing curtains to fit the new window sizes. If the curtains are too long, the quickest and easiest way to alter the length is from the top. Curtains can be lengthened by adding a contrasting or co-ordinating fabric to the bottom of the curtain or as a band a little way up from the bottom. Fabric for the insertion could be patterned for a plain curtain, or vice versa, with each seam trimmed with a toning braid or ribbon. You could also add a frill at the bottom of the curtain made from the same fabric as the insertion.

If you have a pair of curtains that don't go with a window, you could make a decorative rod-pocket curtain.

Shortening curtains

Tack the lining to the curtain fabric below the heading tape, and then cut off the tape. Measure for the new length from the hemline upwards, trimming away any excess material from the top. Purchase new heading tape and apply it following the instructions on page 52.

Lengthening curtains

Purchase sufficient fabric for the depth of the insertion to give you the required curtain length. Allow extra for the seams top and bottom.

1 Undo the lining up the sides of the curtain to just above the proposed cutting line and cut across the curtain.

A quick and easy way to lengthen curtains is to add a plain or contrasting strip to the bottom of the curtain. If possible, use this strip to help co-ordinate the curtain with other furnishings in the room.

2 Place the bottom piece of the curtain and the insertion fabric right sides together with the cut edges aligned. Pin and tack together. Remove the pins and machine stitch. Place the top piece of the curtain to the other cut edge of the insertion, pin, tack and machine stitch as before. Press the seams open.

3 Lengthen the lining by machining a new piece of lining of the required depth to the bottom of the original lining.

Turn up the bottom of the lining by 2.5 cm (1 in) twice and pin it in place. Tack the hem and remove the pins. Machine stitch the hem, press it, and re-sew the lining to the sides of the curtain.

LOOP HEADINGS

Rod-pocket curtains

Cut off the curtain heading, remembering to tack the curtain and lining together just below the cutting line first.

Form a slot heading by making a double turn hem of 10 cm (4 in), pin and tack, removing the pins as you work.

❶ Machine stitch the hem and work a further row of machining 5 cm (2 in) from the first.

❷ Push the rod or pole into the casing formed by the two rows of machining and even out the fullness. For a dress curtain make a tie-back to loop the fullness back.

FOR CURTAINS THAT remain permanently in place, without needing to be drawn, a looped heading is particularly easy to make. It can be used for café curtains and is useful for attaching back rest cushions or headboards to a pole or rod.

For each loop, for the length measure the circumference of the pole and add 7.5 cm (3 in). For the width, the tab should be between 5 cm and 7.5 cm (2 and 3 in). The number of tabs will depend on the length of the pole and the width of the curtain but, as a guide, you will need one at each end, with the remainder spaced at approximately 10 cm to 15 cm (4 to 6 in) intervals.

• Cut a strip of fabric long enough to cut into equal tab lengths and to the width of one tab plus 4 cm (1½ in) seam allowance. Fold the strip in half lengthways, with right sides facing, and stitch the long cut edge. Trim the seam and turn to the right side. Press.

• Cut the required number of tabs from the joined strip of fabric, fold each one in half then pin and tack to the top of the curtain on the right side, with the raw edges even, and the tabs spaced evenly apart.

• To make a facing, cut a 6.5 cm (2½ in) wide strip of fabric to the same width as the curtain and neaten the side and bottom edges. With right sides together, pin and stitch the facing to the curtain top, turn it over to the wrong side and topstitch close to the edge to hold the tabs firmly in place.

Loop headings are very eye-catching – for dress curtains attached to an ornamental rod and café curtains. Fringing and other trimmings add visual impact.

PATTERNS AND TEMPLATES

ANY PATTERN THAT is drawn on a grid in a book or magazine requires to be scaled-up to full size before using. Squared pattern paper is available which is usually printed with dark lines denoting 5 cm (2 in) squares, with lighter lines dividing these into 1 cm (⅜ in) squares. If the diagram only gives half the pattern, follow it precisely as it can be used as a template and placed on a folded piece of paper to cut out as a full pattern.

Enlarging and reducing a pattern
• Count the number of squares across the top of the diagram and down one side. Count the same on the pattern paper. Number the squares along the top from left to right and down the side from top to bottom.

• Place dots where the outline of the shape intersects with a grid line on the printed squares.

• When all the dots have been marked join them up to make the shape. First join any straight lines using a ruler and pencil, for the curved lines join the dots following the shape using a Flexible Curve.

• Cut out the pattern and mark on any instructions printed on the grid diagram, including the seam allowance that will be required when making the item.

• As an alternative to using squared pattern paper, use a tracing or plain pattern paper placed over a cutting board. The printed grid on the board can be seen through either of these papers. When using this method prevent the paper from moving by placing weights at the corners of the paper e.g. books, scissors, etc. DO NOT PIN IN PLACE.

Straight grain line

5 cm
(2 in)

Making a round pattern

• To make a round pattern you will need a piece of square paper the same size as the diameter of the finished item. Fold the piece of paper into four. With a pencil tied to a piece of string, and using one side of the square as the radius, pin the string to the folded point and draw an arc. Cut out the paper circle. For a back piece with a zip, as in the piped round cushion, cut a second circle using the first as a pattern and cut the second one in half where the zip is going to be.

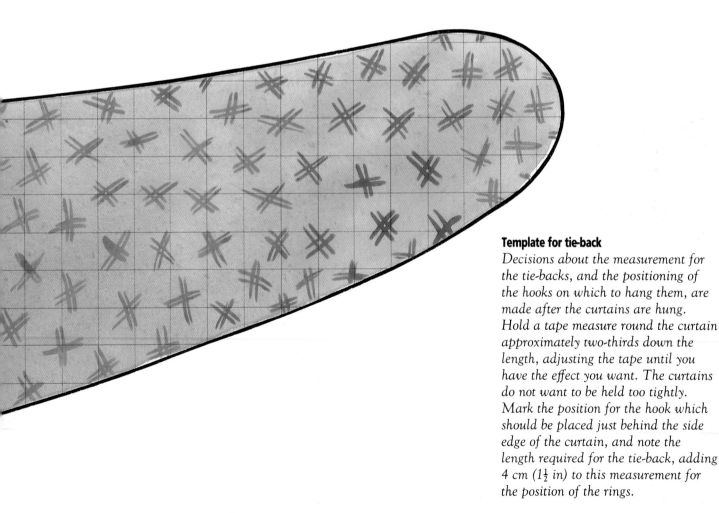

Template for tie-back

Decisions about the measurement for the tie-backs, and the positioning of the hooks on which to hang them, are made after the curtains are hung. Hold a tape measure round the curtain approximately two-thirds down the length, adjusting the tape until you have the effect you want. The curtains do not want to be held too tightly. Mark the position for the hook which should be placed just behind the side edge of the curtain, and note the length required for the tie-back, adding 4 cm (1½ in) to this measurement for the position of the rings.

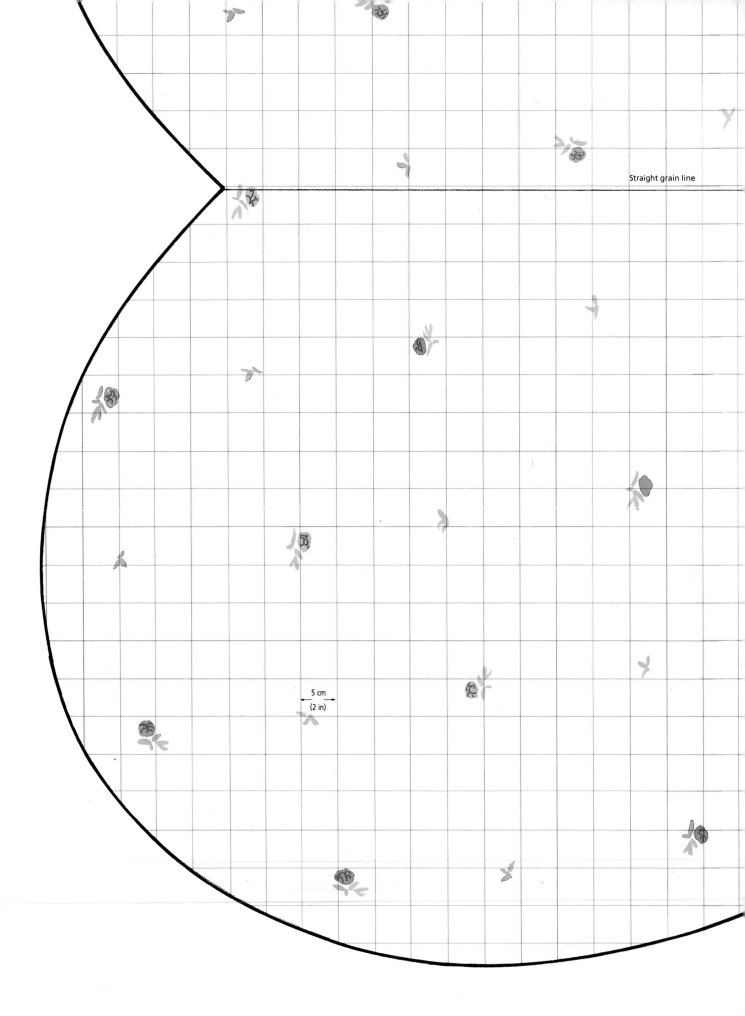

Straight grain line

5 cm
(2 in)

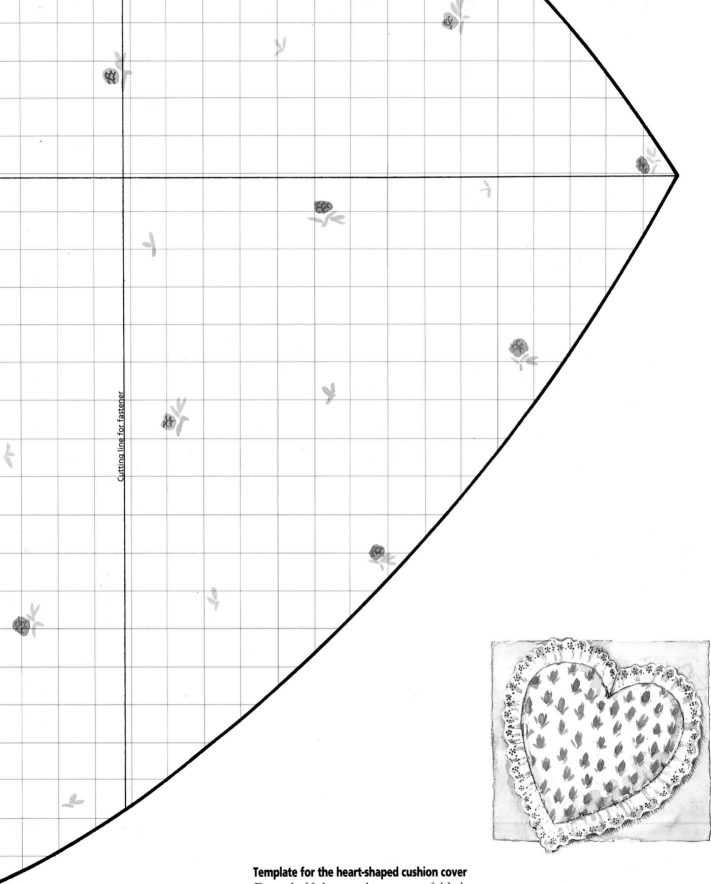

Cutting line for fastener

Template for the heart-shaped cushion cover
Draw half the template onto a folded piece of square paper to the required size, Open out the heart shape pattern and reverse for the back of the cushion.

INDEX

ACKNOWLEDGEMENTS

Quarto would like to thank the following for providing photographs and transparencies, and for permission to reproduce copyright material. While every effort has been made to trace and acknowledge all copyright holders, we would like to apologize should there have been any omissions.

T = top B = bottom L = left R = right TL = top left ML = middle left BL = below left BR = below right MR = middle right

page 2	T	Alexandra Stephenson
page 2	M	Jane Churchill Ltd
page 2	B	fabric: Laura Ashley
page 2 & 3		Calico Lion
page 8		Anna French Ltd
page 9		Laura Ashley
page 10	T	Laura Ashley
page 10	B	Anna French Ltd
page 11		Arthur Sanderson and Sons Ltd
page 12	T	Anna French Ltd
page 12	B	fabric designed by Collier Campbell and distributed by Christian Fischbacher
page 14		Anna French Ltd
page 15	L	Today Interiors
page 15	R	Anna French Ltd
page 16	L	Swish Products Ltd
page 16	R	Rufflette Ltd
page 17		Zoffany
page 18		Anna French Ltd
page 19		Boras Cotton (UK) Ltd
page 20	L	Anna French Ltd
page 20	R	Boras Cotton (UK) Ltd
page 21	L	Rufflette Ltd
page 21	R	Arthur Sanderson and Son Ltd
page 22		Anna French Ltd
page 23		Boras Cotton (UK) Ltd
page 24		Anna French Ltd
page 25		Skopos Design Ltd

page 26		Arthur Sanderson and Son Ltd
page 27	TL	Jane Churchill Ltd
page 27	ML	Jane Churchill Ltd
page 27	BL	Wendy A Cushing
page 27	BR	Skopos Design Ltd
page 27	MR	Anna French Ltd
page 32		Osborne & Little
page 33	L	Laura Ashley
page 33	R	Anna French Ltd
page 34		Boras Cotton (UK) Ltd
page 36		Wesley-Barrell
page 38		Hill & Knowles Ltd
page 39		Rufflette Ltd
page 40		Byron & Byron Ltd
page 43	L	Swish Products Ltd
page 43	R	Osborne & Little
page 45		Osborne & Little
page 47	T	Laura Ashley
page 47	B	Colour Counsellors
page 48		Kirsch/Integra
page 51		Crowson Fabrics
page 53	T	Acrimo/Ibis, Sheffield
page 53	B	Boras Cotton (UK) Ltd/ Stromma

Author's acknowledgements
My sincere thanks to Barbara Carpenter and Mary Straka for their much appreciated practical help with the typing and reading the text.
I thank the following for supplying fabrics to make the step-by-step samples for the projects to be illustrated: Anna French, Monkwell Ltd and Arthur Sanderson & Sons Ltd, and Bernette for allowing the overlocker/serger stitch reference to be used.
I also thank the following suppliers:
Cope and Timmins Ltd (curtain accessories); Newey Goodman Ltd (sewing accessories); C & M Offray and Son Ltd (ribbons); Perivale-Güterman (sewing thread); Rufflette Ltd (curtain heading tapes); Selectus Ltd (Hook and Loop Fastener tape); Vilene Retail (interfacing).

USEFUL ADDRESSES:

Byron & Byron
4 Hanover Yard
off Noel Road
London N1 8BE
071 704 9290

Alexandra Stephenson
Soft Furnishings
15 Reynolds Road
Chiswick
London W4 5AR
081 747 0662

Marion Kaye Curtains
20 Camperdown
Maidenhead
Berks SL6 8DU
0628 70786

Calico Lion/Interfabrics
The Barn,
Randolphs Farm
Brighton Road
Hurstpierpoint
West Sussex BN6 9EL
0273 835166

Osborne & Little
304–308 Kings Road
London SW3 5UH
071 352 1456
For local stockists:
081 675 2255

Arthur Sanderson and Sons Ltd
6 Cavendish Square
London W1M 9HA
071 636 7800

Jane Churchill Ltd
151 Sloane Street
London SW1X 9BX
071 730 6379

Colefax & Fowler
39 Brook Street
London W1Y 2JE
071 493 2231

Stroud Furnishings
152–156 Kentish
Town Road
London NW1 9QD
071 482 4163

Anna French Ltd
343 Kings Road
London SW3 5ES
071 351 1126

Wendy A Cushing
Unit M7
Chelsea Garden Market
Chelsea Harbour
SW10 0X3
071 351 5796

Collier Campbell
2 Clapham Common
Northside
London SW4 0QW
071 720 7862

Laura Ashley
150 Bath Road
Maidenhead
Berkshire SL6 4YS